Snuff out the

The development of flood|

Salford versus Workington Town 5 May 1991 at The Willows.
Traditional floodlights attached to the stand roof.
(Photo: Mike Haddon)

Tom Mather

London League Publications Ltd

Snuff out the Moon
The development of floodlit rugby league

A CIP catalogue record for this book is available from the British Library.

First published in Great Britain in July 2007 by:
London League Publications Ltd, P.O. Box 10441, London E14 8WR

ISBN: 978-1903659-33-5

Cover design by: Stephen McCarthy Graphic Design
                       46, Clarence Road, London N15 5BB

Layout: Peter Lush

Printed and bound by: Biddles Ltd
                       King's Lynn, Great Britain

Foreword

I could, in theory, have watched the Associated Rediffusion's Rugby League Television Trophy in 1955. Although we didn't have a television set, we were living in London, where it was shown and I could have tottered around to more newfangled neighbours. I would probably have been more interested in the adventures of *Rag, Tag and Bobtail* or *Bill and Ben, The Flowerpot Men*.

It would be lying for me to claim any memory of watching television's first floodlit competition. The BBC2 Floodlit Trophy 10 years later was a different matter. That is among my early rugby league memories, all mixed up there with Eddie Waring on a Saturday afternoon.

As Tom Mather points out in this enjoyable book, it was a competition that gave a place in the spotlight to a number of smaller clubs, although it was one of the game's little ironies that Bramley won the Floodlit Trophy in broad daylight, because of the three-day Week.

The other thing that Tom explains is that this was very far from being the start of the story. You have to go back, as he does, to the 1870s and the pioneering days of electric lighting for that.

This isn't just a story about sport. It is also about Victorian entrepreneurship and the battle for hearts and minds.

Think of rugby league now and the chances are that you think of games played at night for television and played, for most months of the season, under lights.

It is illuminating – and how I have tried to avoid that word – to find that the roots of that spectacle go back 130 years and that, then as now, there was a commercial imperative at work.

It is, therefore, good to see Tom back in print, shining a beam into an aspect of the game that would otherwise be neglected. I recommend it – and not necessarily because it is light reading.

Dave Hadfield
The Independent
March 2007

About the author

Tom Mather hails from Lower Ince near Wigan and has supported The Pie-eaters all his life. Until his retirement in 2006 he was a psychology lecturer and part-time freelance rugby league journalist. He has worked for the *Rugby Leaguer, Open Rugby* and more recently *League Weekly*.

He has been involved in rugby league as a player, administrator, supporter and writer, but has a passion for the game's history. His youngest son Barrie-Jon, the former Wigan, Perth and Castleford centre, was the first player to become a dual-code international the wrong way round: he was capped by Great Britain before switching codes to gain an England rugby union cap.

Snuff out the Moon is his fifth book, with a couple more in the pipeline. He now lives with his wife Janet in Lytham on the Fylde Coast and still has a soft spot for The Tigers following his son's two spells with the club.

Acknowledgements

There is no such thing as a one man book, not in today's world. This offering is no different in order for it to see the light of day so to speak a great many people were involved in its production. While I am responsible for the words, the information gathering was in the main done by others.

I would therefore like to express my thanks to them all and in no particular order to the writers of the numerous websites that I consulted while attempting to convert an idea into a reality; secondly to the Siemens Company for providing the initial information that kick-started the book; to the librarians in the reference libraries who unearthed the old newspaper reports quoted in this work at Calderdale Library, Galashields Library, Huddersfield Library, Manchester Library, Salford Library, South Wales Library, Sheffield Library, Woolwich local history archive and Hammersmith & Fulham local history archive; to the editor of *The Dewsbury Reporter*, Graham Morris for his help with the Broughton verses Swinton match, John Riding for his help with the 1955 Floodlit Tournament, Andy Wheelwright the former Blackpool Borough hooker who supplied a massive amount of information regarding the BBC2 Floodlit Competition; Ray French and Neil Fox for their own recollections on the innovation of the four-tackle rule and its inception; David Howes for his memories of events that were to lead to the end of the BBC2 Floodlit Trophy competition.

I would also like to thank Peter Lush for his help with the research in London and thank all those now long-dead reporters of defunct newspapers that covered the match for *The Chorley Guardian, Dewsbury Reporter, Halifax Guardian, Kentish Mercury, Salford Weekly News, Salford Chronicle, Sheffield and Rotherham Independent, Sheffield Daily Telegraph, Sheffield Evening Star and Daily Times, The Monmouthshire Merlin and South Wales Advertiser* and the *Western Mail*. Thanks to Melrose RUFC and Sheffield FC, the world's oldest football club, for their permission to use material in the book.

The extracts from local newspapers covering the Sheffield FC match are reproduced here by kind permission of Sheffield City Libraries who own the copyright. The newspaper reports of the Dewsbury matches are reproduced here by permission of Kirklees Library Authorities.

Thanks to Michael O'Hare for sub-editing, Steve McCarthy for designing the cover, David Williams, Mike Haddon, Alex Service and everyone else who supplied photographs, various rugby league clubs for permission to reproduce programme covers, League Publications for permission to use material from the *Rugby Leaguer*, Peter Lush and Dave Farrar for publishing the book and the staff of Biddles for printing it.

Last, but by no means least, thanks to my wife Janet for proofreading and for the encouragement she gave me.

I hope you enjoy the efforts of all the above-mentioned along with my own to bring you an accurate account of the pioneers who really did try to "Snuff out the Moon".

Tom Mather
June 2007

Contents

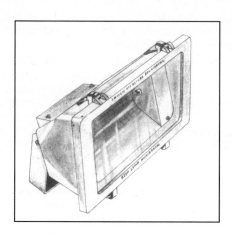

A tungsten iodine floodlight
(Courtesy Alex Service)

One of the Central Park floodlight towers being dismantled on 14 September 1999 following the closure of this famous ground. The site was used for a Tesco supermarket, and the club moved to the JJB Stadium. (Photo: Mike Haddon)

1. Sport and big business

On Saturday 14 October 2006, 72,582 rugby league fans packed into Manchester United FC's Old Trafford stadium for the 2006 Super League Grand Final between St Helens and Hull.

It was a record crowd for the Super League Grand Final, and the third highest for a final to decide the league champions – the 82,067 that squeezed into Odsal in 1960 for the championship final is unlikely ever to be beaten unless Old Trafford is further developed or the match moved to Wembley Stadium.

It was also a record crowd for a floodlit rugby league match in England played in the evening. Under the magnificent Old Trafford lights, the crowd were comfortable in an all-seater stadium, the players were well paid and played their sport full-time, and the game was shown live on Sky television, with highlights on the BBC. Both the competition and the clubs were sponsored, with the corporate facilities at Old Trafford well used.

The match reflected themes that will be examined in this book: the use of floodlights in rugby league; the role of television and the links between sport and big business.

It was very different from the early days of floodlit rugby, when the crowd were not even sure if the lights would work...

It was the philosopher Ludwig Feuerbach, in the early 19th century, who first claimed that man did not understand his own history and as a consequence would remain a prisoner of his own history. Time passes, people pass on, so there is a loss of continuity with the past. Everyone loses track of time, of underestimating just how long ago a player was at this club or that club or when a trophy was won. We tend to think that the continuity is maintained in our society by the written word. That may well be true for statistics, wins, losses, goals or tries scored and such like, particularly those that took place before the advent of the almost instant media we have today.

But events, particularly those in the past, are often written about long after they took place. When history is written - particularly events concerning war - it tends to be the victors who write it. By its very nature it has to be biased. The same is evidently true in sport, sporting innovations are sometimes written about long after their introduction and usually by someone with a vested interest, either in favour of or opposed to the innovation. This was certainly the case during the 19th century when sport was in its embryonic state, developing into the games we know and love today. It is often said that there is nothing new in this world, it

1

has all been done before. The relationship between sport and business is a case in point.

Today in Great Britain there is a battle raging within sport, between sport itself and big business that claims it wants to promote it. Nothing could be further from the truth. Business wants simply to promote business and will do so with whatever means it has at its disposal. Television, particularly satellite television, has long used sport to promote itself. The sale of subscriptions and people buying the sports packages the companies have to offer is balanced against the number of live matches of association football or rugby available to the paying customer. It is obvious that sport and sporting events are used by commercial television companies to attract viewers. Such viewers increase the profitability of the company either through subscriptions or advertising.

They do this simply by buying into the facilities and packages offered by the company and secondly by increasing the numbers viewing the programmes broadcast. The larger the viewing figure, the larger the amount of money the commercial television company can charge for the advertising other companies wish them to broadcast. Those businesses that buy up advertising time from the television companies showing sporting events, generally speaking, see an increase in their business, why else would they do it? Cornhill Insurance was an excellent example. Their sponsorship of test cricket on terrestrial television saw their revenue increase quite dramatically as a result of the exposure.

There is a long history of the relationship between business and sport, dating back to the Victorian era when organised sport was still in its infancy. Sport then was really the domain of the wealthy upper classes and the gentry. Horse racing and prize fighting were common as was hare coursing, cock fighting and fox hunting. A group of wealthy men, the patrons of a particular sport, would join together and form an association. They would sponsor the sport or individuals within that sport. This was common in prize fighting. When these patrons moved on or switched allegiance to another sport the result was not unlike today when a company pulls out of a sponsorship deal with a particular sport.

With the increasing influence of the industrial revolution there came the emergence of a new class of wealthy people, who had made their money from commerce and industry and in attempting to emulate the landed gentry they began to find their own sports to patronise. So new and different sports began to benefit from the sponsorship they introduced.

In the past, boxing matches, cock fighting, cricket matches and so on were often staged on land adjacent to an inn or public house. Indeed it was not unknown for the landlord to actually arrange such events, to increase profits from the drinking carried out by the extra customers. Customers were drawn to the event, and bets were taken on the outcome. Today there are many amateur rugby and association football teams exist in a similar manner by allying themselves to a pub in their immediate area. Both sides profit from the arrangement; the pub with increased profits and the club with somewhere to meet and relax after the match.

Playing sport at night under floodlights is not new, and started for commercial reasons. Ask any avid sports fan of whatever code, association football, rugby union or rugby league, when they think the first floodlit game was actually played. Almost always they will suggest the 1950s. Maybe some will go back to the 1930s. On reflection, this is probably a fair assumption to make as that would be as far back because an individual may well be able to recall from memory. Or it could be as far back as one could reasonably imagine electrical technology capable of lighting a sporting contest becoming available.

Maybe they remember reading somewhere of a match played way back in the 1950s and will automatically assume that it was so long ago it must have been the first one to be played. Whatever reasons they give it must be said that they will come nowhere near the real date.

The first floodlit association football match in the world was actually played in October 1878 and just eight days later the first rugby match was similarly illuminated. Both matches were staged in the north of England. At the time of writing that is now almost 129 years ago. Then electric lighting was in its infancy, so how could this have been achieved? The simple explanation is that it was no different to the reason why television tends to dominate much of sport today - big business, or more precisely the rivalry between big businesses.

Then, as now, the driving force was enterprise within the business field, the only difference is that more than a century ago many other factors came together over a relatively short period of time —perhaps 10 to 20 years. By doing so they allowed an embryonic business to make a giant leap forward. Just what were those factors?

First there was sport itself, whatever sport is chosen as an example. The rugby and association football games were beginning to separate themselves out into the codes and modes of play we know today. The Football Association was formed in London in 1863, the Rugby Football Union in 1871. They did have role models to follow, because both cricket and horse racing had been organised for more than a century. In the 1860s sport was growing fast, organising and battling against each other for the hearts and minds of the young men of the country. These young men were finding themselves with more leisure time and money to spend.

The game of rugby held sway, particularly in many areas in the north of England. It had become extremely popular with working class men who were both playing and watching the game in increasingly greater numbers. Equally, association football was beginning to make its presence felt. Why was this?

Maybe it was due in part to the forward thinking of Queen Victoria who perhaps felt that her subjects were being worked too hard by the many entrepreneurs the Industrial Revolution had and was continuing to generate. More likely, it was due to the pressure society was mounting on the governments of the day - pressure from such as the Chartist movement, early trade unionism and a fear in the minds of many in authority that the French Revolution and its aftermath was still fresh in the minds of the general population.

Whatever the reasons, Parliament passed many laws and reforms during her reign. The Ten Hour Act of 1847 reduced the number of hours youngsters could work. The 1850 Factory Act was aimed at women and children and effectively banned them from working after 2 o'clock on a Saturday afternoon. This had a knock-on effect. Factory owners realised that once the women and children stopped working, the men remaining were unable to be fully productive and so it was better to let all the workers finish at the same time. Over the next 20 years or so a number of amendments to the Act freed more and more workers on a Saturday afternoon to do as they wanted. Thus the working classes had for the first time, leisure, and leisure on a day other than Sunday, which was still then considered to be 'the Lord's Day'.

During this period factory owners created sports facilities for their workers and even sponsored teams. They did so in the hope of obtaining the goodwill of their workers. The masses used this time and the new facilities to partake in the sport of their choice, be it rugby or association football.

From around the 1870s onward there was a change in attitude towards the nation's health. This attempted to encourage people to lead a healthy and moral lifestyle because it was felt such an approach would lead to a more disciplined workforce. Something was desperately needed if the industrial revolution was to maintain pace and impetus. There was the development of public parks in the towns, libraries, museums and even public baths were introduced. Within this new approach sport was encouraged.

Both association football and rugby began to prosper, develop and expand their horizons. The downside of this, particularly in the north of England, was that supporters of particular clubs began to become more and more demanding. This was in response to many clubs, particularly rugby clubs, that had cashed in on the new-found leisure time, by enclosing their grounds and making people pay to watch their sport. Suddenly it was not enough to play the game, winning also became important, as did entertaining the paying spectators. People were not going to part with their hard earned cash to watch a losing team. Nowhere was this more evident than in the north of England within the rugby fraternity. Association football was not far behind, and would adopt a more sensible attitude to developing their sport that was ultimately to see it become the country's premier sport.

The country saw a massive swing toward spectator sports by the 1860s and both association football and rugby were to the forefront. The explosion in railway development also played its part. Players and supporters were better able to travel around the country. Clubs could play matches further and further afield as the transport system developed.

There were also other forces at work that were far removed from the sports field. These were originally in the field of science but by the 1860s were entering commerce and business.

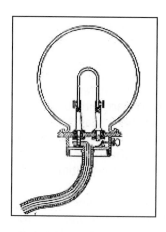

Top: The lamp invented by William Staite. This is a much simpler version of an arc lamp and keeping the gap between the two carbon rods was much more difficult than with Serrin's version.

Right: Staite produced the forerunner for the arc lamps produced later by Serrin and Jablochkov. The only power source available to him was by batteries. These were expensive to run so Staite's business failed, not because his invention did not work, but simply it was too expensive to run.

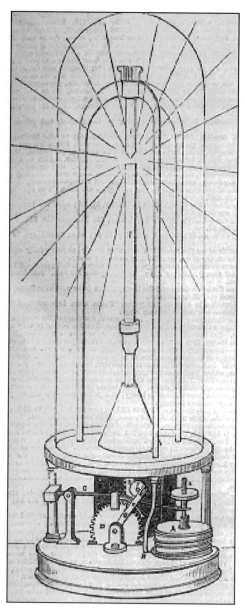

2. Developing electricity

It was the two forces of business and commerce allied to manufacturing that had driven the Industrial Revolution forward in Britain. These had capitalised upon the original power sources that had kick-started the revolution in the first place, water power and then steam, which initially steam provided more consistent power than water. Steam turned the machinery that drove the revolution relentlessly onward. Later gas helped maintain the momentum of the revolution.

There was a new energy source also existing around this period, electricity. Electricity was not a new source of power, of course, knowledge of its existence dates back to ancient times and it was being written about as early as the sixth century BC. It was, however, in the 1800s that progress in actually producing useable electricity began to accelerate. Two men were to exercise a massive influence on both the progress and speed at which the knowledge was to develop. The first, Werner von Siemens was a German engineer the other was the Belgium engineer, Zenode Gramme. Both were working simultaneously on developing an electrical dynamo. It was the rivalry between these two that was to drive forward this new source of power as they both strived to produce the best dynamo in what was a fast growing area of development.

By 1867 Siemens had completed his work on the dynamo, or more correctly speaking an electromagnetic generator. For the very first time there was a reasonably reliable method of producing electricity. This generator ironically, while producing the newest form of energy, was in fact driven by one of the oldest - steam. Just three years later Gramme developed his own dynamo-electric machine which improved on Siemens's; once again driven by a steam engine. The problem was that steam engines tended to be monstrous in size and only produced around 60 revolutions per minute, which was far too slow. The dynamos of the time needed to rotate at around 900 revolutions per minute if they were to produce any electrical power. A cumbersome system of belts and pulleys were needed to convert the lumbering speed of the steam engine into the dynamo's required rate.

Help was at hand, however. By the 1870s a new smaller generation of steam engine capable of rotating at around 600 revolutions per minute were being developed and becoming more readily available. These had been developed for use in sawmills and also for the threshing machines coming into use on farms. Such machines needed to operate at a much faster speed than the existing steam engine. The other vital bonus as far as electricity development was concerned was that they were smaller. They had to be, because they needed to be transported from field to field quickly and easily. These new second-generation steam engines added to the rapidly developing dynamos available, produced reasonably portable electrical energy. Both the dynamo and the steam engine were now transportable with relative ease. There were just a couple more problems to be solved.

The first of these was simply how could the electrical energy generated by the dynamo be transported across long distances. The solution to this was found quite by accident in 1873 at the international Vienna Universal Exhibition. An engineer called Fontaine, who was in partnership with Zenode Gramme, was in charge of the stand used to advertise Gramme's discoveries, products and their uses. On the stand were two dynamos, one was used to provide the electrical current for the stand. The other was being held in reserve in case the first should break down.

By chance, one of the workmen connected the two dynamos together by mistake. The second dynamo, which was not being used to produce current, immediately came to life. Fontaine instantly recognised the importance of the discovery and began a series of impromptu experiments. He asked the workman to lengthen the connecting cables by varying degrees; each time the result was the same. Eventually the two dynamos were around 250 metres apart but when the two were connected, the second still immediately sprung to life. Quite by accident Fontaine had solved the problem of how to transport electrical energy over long distances. More importantly what it also meant was that Fontaine had provided the long sought after electric motor and coupled this with a simple means of transporting this electrical energy over large distances.

Now the question was how to turn this new form of energy into a usable form. Most engineers were considering electricity for use in illumination. The rival gas companies were in the lead, simply because they were fast illuminating every street and house in the land. Gaslight seemed to brighten everyone's life and as such was constantly in the minds of the population. If electricity was ever to make a breakthrough as a source of power then it would have to be brought to the attention of people in the same way gas was. It would have to be used to illuminate people's lives.

There were a number of methods proposed to produce a suitable illumination force to light up the gloom, but the first practical way of doing this bore no relationship to the light bulbs we know today. This first illuminating device was in reality nothing more than an open flame. It was known as the arc lamp. Its operation was simple and had been known for more than 50 years. In fact the principle had first been demonstrated in 1804 by Sir Humphrey Davy, at the Royal Society in London. Two carbon rods were placed in a line with each other, end to end. Each rod was connected to a different pole on the electrical supply. The electricity was switched on and the carbon rods slowly brought closer and closer together until they touched. When this happened the circuit was complete and electricity flowed through it. In so doing, the current flow caused the tips of the carbon rods to heat up and glow. The carbon rods were then slowly pulled apart until a spark of electricity jumped or arced across the gap. This arcing in turn caused carbon rods to heat up even more until they were so hot that the carbon began to vaporize.

It was this vaporized carbon that became incandescent and in so doing produced an intense blue-white light, which was so strong it lit up the gloom. The major problem with this form of lighting was that the two carbon rods were not used up at the same rate. When a direct current was used the positive carbon rod was burned away at twice the rate of the negative rod. An alternating current on the other hand tended to equalise the consumption of each of the rods. The problem was to ensure the gap between the two rods remained constant to ensure a reliable light source. If the gap became too large or too small it caused the heat to drop, the carbon ceased to vaporise as readily and so the light faded.

After its discovery in the very early 1800s, arc-lamp development over the next 60 years or so centred around discovering a means of simply and reliably automatically adjusting the gap between the two carbon rods, to ensure a constant intensity of light. The system of arc lighting that seems to have been favoured in this country was the Serrin Lamp, named after its French inventor. Using the Serrin system the two carbon rods were maintained at a constant distance apart by an elaborate clockwork mechanism connected to the topmost of the two rods. The clockwork mechanism worked in conjunction with the rate of wear on the carbon rods. It was a system which was used in a large number of lighthouses scattered around the British coastline.

Serrin was not the only one to produce a clockwork mechanism to operate an arc light. Similar work had been done years earlier by the Englishman, William Staite. Way back in 1834 Staite had produced a mechanism that would keep the gap between two carbon rods at a constant distance. So successful was his mechanism that it had been used in 1848 to floodlight the National Gallery in London. He introduced the public to electric lighting and they had become used to such demonstrations. Sadly Staite was a little too advanced, because at the time the only electrical power source available was provided by batteries. These were expensive to run and when his company failed, he faded away, and never received the accolade his work deserved.

By the 1870s a more reasonably reliable method of achieving the feat of maintaining the gap between the carbon rods was readily available. This had been possible due to the efforts of the Russian engineer Paul Jablochkov. He had been the director of telegraphs between Moscow and Kursk. In 1875 he resigned his position in an attempt to further his education. He left Russia intending to travel to America to visit the International Exhibition in Philadelphia. He only got as far as Paris. There he met Louis Breguet, who had developed a telegraph system for the French navy along with electric clocks for use on board ship. It seems both had a common interest.

Taking a shine to the Russian, Breguet offered him the use of his laboratory. Jablochkov took up the offer and by 1876 had developed the Jablochkov candle. It would revolutionise the use of the electric arc lamp because it was simpler, cheaper and more reliable. It did not have the complicated clockwork mechanisms of previous lamps. Having developed an interest in arc-lamp technology, Jablochkov moved away from the conventional approach to solve the problem of maintaining the gap between the two carbon rods. The carbon rods in his lamp were mounted upright and parallel to each other rather than vertical and facing each other end to end. The gap between the two was kept constant by inserting a piece of inert material such as plaster of Paris. The secret was that the inert material burned away at the same rate as the carbon in the rods. This ensured that the gap between the two remained constant at all times. This simple change removed the need for a complex Serrin clockwork mechanism to regulate the gap caused by erosion.

Thus the light source also remained relatively constant. The whole was then encased in a glass sphere which made the device safer, because the flame was kept behind glass. The only problem was that once the rods were burned down a new set of rods had to be inserted and the candle lit once again. As each candle lasted around 90 minutes, this could cause problems. However replacements could be fitted in minutes. By the mid-1870s everything was in place for the use of electricity to take off.

There were a number of rival companies striving to develop and improve their own version of the electric motor. Siemens, Gramme and Thomas Edison, the famous American inventor, were busy working in this field. In Europe the competition between Siemens and Gramme was pushing forward the development and efficiency of the electric motor with great speed. The two companies were rivals and desperately trying to be first to gain a foothold in the new marketplace they were attempting to create.

Technology was also improving the efficiency of the arc-lamp system. With a relatively reliable power source along with a similarly reliable illumination method, the Jablochkov candle, and the means to transport electrical energy over larger and larger distances using copper wires, everything was in place for electricity to surge ahead. The problem was that the British were a suspicious lot, particularly when it came to electricity. This was surprising given the innovations that were being developed in the country then. An accurate estimate of the feeling of the time would be, "if it's not broken don't fix it." The lighting system that existed in the country was perfectly adequate, the envy of the world in fact, why then was electricity needed? Equally, the gas companies had a monopoly and were not going to give it up without a fight. Allied to that, the coal industry saw the gas companies as the best customers for their product so they were also reluctant to embrace this new energy source. There is little doubt that they looked unfavourably on a new rival power industry developing. Given the powerful lobbying available to the gas and coal industries the electrical companies faced an uphill struggle to make an impact on society. How could they break the powerful stranglehold exerted by gas and coal?

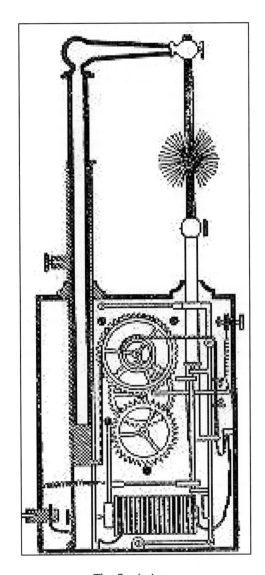

The Serrin Lamp

This used a very complex and complicated
system of gears to ensure that
the two carbon rods were kept at a
constant distance apart thus
ensuring the brightest possible 'arc' light

3. Floodlights arrive

By 1878 it appeared that the various electrical companies springing up had devised a suitable strategy to achieve the aim of breaking the domination of the gas companies. They could not hope to knock the gas companies off their perch by illuminating the streets of the cities and towns. Councils that had been investing in street lighting had done so using gas. Gas was in place and working so there was no incentive for the authorities to change the situation. More and more houses were also being illuminated by gas. The gas was supplied to houses through pipes installed by the gas companies. People were used to it, considered it not to be dangerous and had no knowledge of electricity.

On the other hand electric arc-lamps were considered to be too expensive and risky to install into an average family home. The light produced was far too bright and would dazzle people and the almost naked flame was a fire hazard. So there was no incentive for the electricity companies to enter that market. It was true that some progressive factory owners had commissioned electric arc-lamps to be fitted in their factories, the intention being to improve the illumination for their workers who worked night shifts. They had gone to the expense of purchasing their own Gramme or Siemens engine or even batteries to produce the electricity needed. But these factory owners were few and far between in those early days of electricity.

There had been some successes using the Jablochkov candle to light up streets, docks and public buildings. In 1878 the Metropolitan Board of Works in London had used electricity and Jablochkov candles to light up the Victoria Embankment. Also the City of London had installed similar lighting at Billingsgate Fish Market. Such endeavours were few and far between and were regarded as novelties rather than a practical lighting system. If the electrical companies wanted to make an impact then it would not come from attempting to persuade people in authority to switch from lighting streets by gas, to electric light. Such a strategy would lead to a long slow battle of attrition against a powerful and well-established enemy. A different approach was called for.

It was then that the electricity companies in this country hit upon the perfect vehicle, or so they thought, to advertise their new product: sport. Then as now, it seems, to promote a product, it is one of the best vehicles available. Both rugby and association football were beginning to attract followers in large numbers. In 1877 the Yorkshire County Rugby Union had sanctioned the sport's first cup competition, the Yorkshire Challenge Cup. Sixteen senior clubs in the county had been invited to compete for the trophy. The competition was played over four consecutive Saturdays in December that year. The final was staged on the Saturday between Christmas and New Year 1877.

It was an enormous success, not just from a playing perspective but also in the number of spectators it attracted to the ties. The idea of a cup final was not new; the Football Association had sanctioned such a competition back in 1871, the FA Cup. That competition had proved very successful for the association football code and its popularity was still growing as the decade was coming to its close. Rugby's Yorkshire Cup, however, eclipsed even that competition for the number of supporters it attracted.

That fact would not have been lost on the electricity companies, equally they would have noted the vast newspaper coverage the event attracted and the impact it had in Yorkshire. The coverage had been extensive; some in the press supported the venture, while others decried it as a step down the road to professionalism in rugby. Whichever standpoint was taken, the result was exactly the same - publicity. What better way was there to sell this new product to the British public?

The electricity companies would do what the gas companies could not do; they would allow the masses to watch their sport at night. They would light up the night sky to such an extent that rugby and association football matches could be played.

When Chorley Rugby Club were about to stage such a match under the newly named floodlights, the local reporter of the time coined a phrase which today would be an advertisers' dream. He wrote that the club were attempting "To snuff out the moon". That was just what the electricity companies were attempting to do, to put out the moon's light and replace it with man-made light. A short time later the Brush Company in America placed their arc-lights in a glass sphere and described them as "Miniature moons on carbon points held captive in glass globes". However the lights were described, the electric companies were going to attempt to light up the night sky using them.

The gas companies appear to have been unconcerned by the growth in the knowledge of electricity and the attempts to make inroads into their territory. Around this time an article in the *Journal of Gas Lighting* was scathing of the new electricity systems sprouting up around the country. It said: "Electricity may be the champagne light of fête days, but coal gas light is the bass beer light of everyday life."

The implication made was a simple one, electricity produced a system of lighting that was of no substance, and consequently it was not a threat to gas. True, electricity had novelty value and the electrical companies were simply cashing in on the novelty value of their product. However, they believed that gas was never going to be replaced by electricity and consequently the gas companies were unperturbed by the new phenomena.

It is unclear if the strategy adopted by the electricity companies was arrived at by consensus and consultation between themselves. It is more likely to assume that the original idea was the brainchild of one or perhaps a couple of companies. Once the idea hit the public domain, others simply followed suit. The evidence available covering the first ever floodlit association football match suggests that the owner of the Sheffield company supplying the lighting apparatus just happened also to be a keen sportsman. Also he just happened to be connected with the football club staging that event. It is likely that this was the case in other parts of the country and with other sports. However, the tremendous amount of activity all around the country in a relatively short space of time involving the use of electricity to light sporting events would suggest some collusion between the various electrical companies. On the other hand it could have been the companies such as Siemens and Gramme, makers of the electric dynamo machines that were driving the whole thing forward. They were in a better position to do that, as the small companies moving into this new technology would need to purchase their dynamos from one or other of these companies.

It does not matter which was the case, for as the 1878-79 rugby and association football seasons opened there was a plethora of floodlit games being arranged by clubs of both persuasions. The rugby code was, by far, the more likely choice for the companies, especially in the north of England than the south. It was there that the sport was attracting large numbers of supporters. In Sheffield the association football code was chosen simply because of the interest in that code held by John Tasker. He was first and foremost a cricket lover and as the cricket club had been instrumental in forming an association football club, he became a follower of that game rather than the rugby code.

The electrical companies still had a dilemma, they had to marry up the existing electrical technology with the demands placed upon them by the sport they were attempting to light. The approach adopted was more trial and error than sound judgement. From the newspaper reports of those days it is clear that sometimes the companies got it right, but at other times horribly wrong.

They certainly predicted correctly the measure of interest the supporters had in such ventures. They turned up in their thousands to witness their sport played at night. A constant theme running through all of these floodlit matches was that the clubs badly underestimated the interest such events would generate. Thousands also turned up to simply witness and marvel at the new electric lighting. They were then able to say that they had been there when the lighting had been in operation.

More importantly many of those who turned out to observe the lighting rather than the sport were very influential in the business and commerce world. This was just what the electrical companies must have hoped for: to influence people and educate them about the possibilities this new energy source offered. People in authority who turned up to watch could not fail to have been influenced by the reaction of the thousands of ordinary people watching the miracle of association football or rugby being played at night.

One other thing the electrical companies judged to perfection was the attitude of the sporting clubs, particularly the rugby clubs of the north. Given that the companies were going to provide illumination of the game, usually at no cost, or for a very small part of the revenue obtained, clubs readily accepted the invitation of getting 'something for nowt'.

Various clubs claimed to have been the first to stage a floodlit match, but the honour of staging the first rugby match under such lighting fell to Lancashire. In association football it was their rivals from across the Pennines, Yorkshire, that claimed the honour. The association football club was Sheffield FC while the rugby honour went to Broughton, a Salford-based club. Broughton pipped Chorley to the post, but not without feathers being ruffled on both sides.

This simple fact of being the first caused other problems, arising from the newspapers' attitude. They were the only means of mass communication. While the first floodlit game would have been very newsworthy, was the second one going to be as newsworthy? It would seem the hard-nosed newspaper editors of the time, like today, thought not. Coverage in the press of such events became progressively less as the frequency of such matches increased. Even reporters fell into two camps, those favouring the new venture - even if they highlighted the failures - and those who did not. So, all did not run smoothly with this new venture, as is often the case when sport, business and technology are combined.

Some companies successfully lit up rugby or association football matches while others had a disaster. But the old maxim of 'there is no such thing as bad publicity,' was true here. Electric light was being reported in the newspapers and talked about by the workers and captains of industry. The gas companies now had a fight on their hands but had not yet realised it. The rapid increases in the technology associated with electricity would soon make them sit up and take notice. It was a battle they would lose and a major reason was the input from sport.

4. Association football

The new electrical companies sought to advertise the potential of the new source of energy via the medium of sport. The question is, just how did the sports they attempted to utilise get to the point where they were able to attract the attention of the rapidly evolving electricity companies? Obviously a business is not going to invest in something that is not well supported, there would be no point. Businesses, after all, are not charitable institutions. Especially during that period, when the industrial revolution was at its height and with the work ethic prevailing at the time, business was considerably more exploitative than it is today.

Rugby and association football were attracting massive amounts of support from the public, particularly from the working classes. And they had done so over a relatively short time.

In May 1857, two Sheffield cricketers, William Prest and Nathaniel Creswell, both former pupils at Harrow School, were discussing ways in which they could keep themselves and their teammates fit during the long winter months. They felt if they could keep their fitness levels high it would give them an advantage, particularly in the early part of the cricket season. After much discussion they concluded that association football would help them achieve this, rather than rugby. Maybe their thinking was that association football offered less chance of a player being injured or even killed as sometimes happened at that time in rugby, as hacking could lead to players being kicked in the head.

In those days association football was not particularly well established and often there would be teams of up to 20-a-side contesting matches. Those matches often went on until darkness descended and players could no longer see the ball. There was another problem: because of the different rules people played by, not just from town to town but even in different parts of a town.

Sheffield Football Club had its first headquarters in a potting shed and greenhouse at the bottom of a garden in East Bank Road. In October 1857, Creswell became secretary and captain of the new outfit.

The first task for the club officials was to study the many different sets of rules that were used in football. From their deliberations they then drew up a set of rules for their club. These rules appear to have become the cornerstone of the future football rules that were to become commonly accepted and influenced the rules adopted by the Football Association.

Prest and Creswell must have got something right, for the club attracted a vast amount of interest in the city of Sheffield. It grew rapidly and soon members began to form teams among themselves, single men verses married men or professional men verses tradesmen, just to allow them to play the game. The idea snowballed, and in just five short years there were some 15 separate clubs playing the game within Sheffield and the surrounding area. When the Football Association was formed in London it gave rise to the formation of the Sheffield Football Association. Sheffield FC became founder members of it and are members to this day. The Sheffield club is credited with being the oldest football club in the world as well as being responsible for many of the innovations that have made the game what it is today. This was recognised in 2004 when FIFA awarded the Sheffield club its Order of Merit for services to the game. They are in very exalted company, as the only other club with such an honour is the great Real Madrid club in Spain.

During the early years of their existence the Sheffield club was responsible for a number of innovations that are taken for granted in the modern game. They were the first club to use a crossbar on its goalposts. In the early days the posts normally consisted of two wooden uprights across which a piece of rope was strung. Sheffield replaced the rope with a solid piece of wood. Also by 1875 they had incorporated heading the ball into the way the game was played. When the club travelled down to London and started to kick the ball high across the goalmouth and their players leapt up to try to head it towards the goal, the watching spectators fell about roaring with laughter.

Given the club's reputation for innovation within the game of association football, it was not totally unexpected that the electricity companies should target Sheffield as a possible candidate to host the first ever recorded floodlit association football match. It was a large city where rugby was not really the major sport and there were a good many players and supporters of the game. The sport, like the new electricity companies, was ripe for further development. Everything was in place within the city. And it may have helped that a member of the Sheffield Cricket Club which had spawned the football club, owned an electricity company. Not only that but he was a man with a reputation for innovation himself, albeit within the business community.

Once association football became more formalised and the FA came into being, the game grew rapidly. In 1871 with the introduction of the FA Cup for association football clubs there was a great upturn in the game's fortunes. The FA Cup steadily attracted more and more clubs wanting to compete for it, even the top Scottish clubs entered the competition. This one competition helped spread the game further and further across the country. There can be no doubt that this rapid development was the catalyst which attracted the electrical companies to target association football, as a game which could be used to bring electricity to the attention of the working man. By 1878 the game was firmly established as a major sport throughout the country. It was attracting large crowds, sometimes rivalling those watching rugby. The electricity companies had at least one vehicle to which they could hitch their light, as the decade was coming to a close.

The Siemens Dynamo

Werner von Siemens   William Siemens
(Both pictures courtesy Siemens Ltd)

5. Rugby football

Although the newer association football code had made rapid developments during the 1870s, particularly after splitting from the rugby code, rugby itself had made even greater strides. In the north, in particular, rugby football had captured the imagination of the working man. Given their newly won leisure time on a Saturday afternoon they had begun to flock in their thousands to watch or play the game of rugby. All however, was not well. It is true that the Rugby Football Union (RFU) was formed in 1871 but it had been formed in London, by London based clubs. It was a fact which rankled with the northern clubs who, while outnumbering their southern counterparts, never felt they were part of the decision-making process. They felt that much of the time the tail was wagging the dog.

There was still another strand to this growing divide: the spectators. In the south the game was watched by the proverbial one man and his dog, but the same was not true in the north. Many northern clubs had enclosed their grounds and charged spectators an entry fee to watch the games. It was a double-edged sword. The paying punters demanded more from their club - winning every match for a start. They also wanted to see the best players playing the game, at their ground, preferably for their club.

As the game progressed during the 1870s the supporters began to grow restless and tired of the seemingly endless round of friendly games that comprised rugby fixtures. They were beginning to pick and choose the matches that they spent their hard-earned cash on to watch. A local derby would result in a full house as bragging rights were also at stake, while other matches were beginning to be played before partially filled grounds.

The alarm bells were ringing and it was the senior clubs in both Lancashire and Yorkshire that were responding to the crisis as they saw it. The Yorkshire senior clubs applied to their county body for permission to set up their own league. The authorities in the capital were appalled by the idea, feeling it was yet another step down that evil road to professionalism. They still could not grasp the competitive nature of the game in the north. The suggestion was turned down by both the Yorkshire County RU under pressure from the south, and the RFU itself. It must be said that both the county body and the clubs were far from happy with the situation but felt that there was more than one way to skin a cat.

In 1877 the Yorkshire County RU decided to launch the Yorkshire County Cup Competition. Entry in this first ever rugby cup competition was by invitation of the authorities.

Such a competition was not unknown in England: as mentioned earlier the Football Association in 1871 had launched its own competition for the FA Cup. This had sparked a massive upsurge in interest in the game of association football from both clubs and supporters. It could be argued in some ways that this competition was responsible for the formation of the professional Football League in 1888. The FA Cup had thrown up ties between teams that would not normally meet each other in competition. Equally it saw teams who were strictly amateur, competing against teams who were not. There is little doubt that the Yorkshire Cup competition had a similar effect on the game of rugby.

It was in this area that the differing approach of the rugby and association football authorities is best highlighted. The FA after debating the problem for four years reluctantly accepted that professional players were a legitimate part of the sport. They did not set up a witch hunt to drive professionalism out of association football. On the contrary, in 1885 they sanctioned professionalism - clubs and players were left free to go down whichever road they wished without hindrance from the governing body. But the rugby code continued to attack professionalism with a zeal and enthusiasm which was bound to lead to confrontation. In the eyes of the authorities cup rugby was competitive rugby and competitive rugby equalled professional rugby. That was the Rugby Football Union's stance, that taking part in the sport was reward in itself and no other reward was necessary. They could, however, find no reason to veto the cup competition. So the Yorkshire clubs at least now had meaningful competitive matches, if only during the month of December.

There is little doubt that the first Yorkshire Cup was an unqualified success, the players loved the competition, particularly the winners who picked up a gold medal for their efforts. The spectators turned up in their thousands to watch the ties so they were obviously pleased and consequently so were the clubs who gladly pocketed their share of the large gate receipts. The first final was watched by a reputed 15,000 crowd, far higher than those who watched the FA Cup final. More importantly the press loved the competition, and coverage was enormous at both local and national level. What better vehicle could the electricity companies have to advertise their product? They could reach tens of thousands of people at one event - a rugby match or an association football match. They could then reach many thousands more when they read about the event in the newspapers. All that was needed was to persuade a club to play a game, any sort of game, at night.

So it would seem, as 1878 dawned, that all the elements required to make such an event possible came together: a reliable and easily transportable electric motor; a reliable light source, the Jablochkov candle; a means of transporting electrical energy over fairly long distances and finally sport. Sport, the vehicle that was attracting large numbers of people to one place at the same time. It was perfect, what could go wrong? The electricity companies certainly did not think anything would or could.

They had prepared well and absorbed lots of the information that was available to them, particularly on the sporting side of the equation. They quickly realised that any game that was to be floodlit would need to be a local derby of some description. Given the transport situation in 1878, travelling any fairly long distance would prove difficult, if not impossible.

The railways were good, but not that good. Travel was difficult enough at weekends during the winter months, but trying to travel on a weekday evening was very difficult indeed.

Spectators, the very people the companies were out to impress would not have finished work until 6pm or even later and needed to be back at work the following morning by around 7.30am. Therefore they would be unwilling or unable to travel any great distance. What the companies did not want was the expense of staging an event only for very few spectators to show up to witness the spectacle. Their rivals, the gas companies, would gain great pleasure from that. They also realised very early on that if they were to get the agreement from clubs they needed it would be because they, not the clubs, would be footing the bill. Or, if not, that it would be a case of both parties profiting from a share of the gate receipts.

So even though at first it appeared that the whole country was available to the electricity companies for their enterprise, this was not the case. They needed a large conurbation, preferably a city, and within that area they needed two teams which attracted large support and were close enough together to generate fierce local rivalry between the fans, which would cause the supporters to turn out for the game. This reduced quite considerably the possibilities available for such events. Certainly rugby, particularly in the north, offered greater opportunities to the electricity companies than did association football, simply because there were more clubs and they attracted greater attendance at their matches.

Another problem the companies faced was that once it became known in the rugby and association football fraternities just what they were trying to achieve, they would been swamped with offers to host the first match. But clubs may well not have been so keen to host the second or third such match.

In Lancashire rugby circles there is no doubt that a row raged between the Broughton club based in Salford and the fledgling upstart Chorley club from near Bolton for the honour of being the first to stage a floodlit match. On the other side of the Pennines in Sheffield, Sheffield FC probably also had a fight on its hands, particularly from the Hallam club, reputed to be the second oldest in the world. Certainly both clubs would have wanted to take part in the game but only if it was staged at their own ground. They were not going to surrender glory to a near neighbour. Sheffield FC however, had a secret weapon in the form of a benefactor who was both powerful and well connected.

The electricity companies needed to select carefully the venues they would choose. Not only was the number of supporters attending the match important, they also needed to attract as many businessmen and influential people in the area to the game. Probably as important, if not more so, was the interest the press would have in the event.

What would be the best time to stage such an event? Did the club involved have their matches covered by the local weekly newspaper as well as a local daily? Ideally the electricity companies would like both to be there because that meant more coverage and more readers. Would the national newspapers cover such an event? If they did then the resulting publicity would be a smack in the eye for the gas companies.

They eventually settled on Manchester and Sheffield as the two cities that would provide the venues for the first ever recorded floodlit association football and rugby matches in the world. There is also little doubt that their choice proved to be correct, certainly in the case of Sheffield. The publicity generated at the Manchester event seems not to have been quite as generous. The company involved in lighting the rugby match there seemed to lack the business acumen and flair for publicity of those involved in Sheffield.

However, there was one thing that had not been factored into the equation by any of the electricity companies. It was to have a detrimental effect on the whole grand scheme. The factor was simply, the weather.

6. The first floodlit match

The first recorded floodlit association football to be played anywhere in the world was staged at Bramall Lane in Sheffield. By 1878 the ground already had a long sporting history, first coming into use as a sports ground 24 years earlier. In 1854, six local cricket clubs had rented the site from the Duke of Norfolk. One of those clubs was the Wednesday Cricket Club, which had been formed in 1820. One of their members was instrumental in staging the floodlit game.

The first cricket match was played on the ground in 1855 and by 1863 it had become the headquarters of Yorkshire County Cricket Club. Bramall Lane quickly became the sporting focus of the city.

The first association football match to be played on the ground was staged on 29 December 1862, when Sheffield FC met Hallam in a holiday fixture. The present Sheffield Wednesday Club made its debut at the ground in 1868. However, it was not just association football and cricket which were to use the sporting facilities of Bramall Lane; bowls, lacrosse and tennis were regularly played there and there was a cinder running track laid out around the outside of the association football pitch. In 1874 the ground had even staged a baseball game, when the Boston Reds met the Philadelphia Blues in an exhibition game. The cricket committee which ran the ground while accepting that there would be damage to the cricket pitch by these other sporting activities felt that the rental income they gained more than adequately compensated them.

So it was no surprise that a floodlit association football match staged in Sheffield would gravitate to Bramall Lane. The driving force behind the organisation of the event was John Tasker. He was both a pioneer electrical engineer and a member of the Wednesday Cricket Club. No doubt he would have preferred to light up a cricket match but the logistics of such a feat were beyond the scope of electrical technology at that time. So it was that he settled for lighting up an association football match and John Tasker, Sons and Company were given the task.

Tasker was no stranger to challenging situations such as that presented by this enterprise. His business interests in Sheffield had begun in the boot and shoe making industry. He later added an engineering department to his factory and was responsible for patenting a machine capable of grinding armour plating. This in turn led to the company at one time having a monopoly on the manufacture of armour plating for the Royal Navy, which also led to him becoming very wealthy. It was said that 'adaptability' was

25

his middle name and his company turned out a wide variety of products, from bouncy rubber balls to a new method of repairing galoshes using India rubber.

It was his involvement with rubber that was eventually to lead him into the fledgling electricity industry. He saw electricity as the power source of the future and also quickly spotted an opening providing the insulation of electrical cables used to carry the new source of energy. He saw the opportunity offered to his company by electricity and took it. He was therefore in a position to further his business interests when the opportunity arose to light up the night sky and allow association football to be played.

He remained a firm believer in electrical power and also in the new invention by Alexander Graham Bell, the telephone. In later life he was responsible for developing the first ever telephone exchange in the city of Sheffield which, at its inception, had only 12 subscribers. He was also involved in building the first power station in the city and laying electrical cabling into people's houses. He was a man of vision; luckily he was also a keen sportsman.

Tasker combined his limited electrical knowledge with his sporting knowledge of association football to decide how to light the field of play. He decided the best way would be to light the ground from behind the goal lines. By doing this he was breaking the field down into two halves and was lighting each one independently. Also he realised that by lighting the pitch in this manner the brighter light would be in the goalmouth areas where hopefully most of the action would take place. It is true that the lighting would be at its poorest on the halfway point of the pitch but he felt that very little action would normally occur in this area.

He realised, as well, that by lighting in this way it freed both sides of the pitch for the spectators to watch the match. His plan was to light each half of the field using two arc-lamps in the form of Jablochkov candles. Behind each candle he would place a large reflector to focus the light down onto the playing surface. He decided to place two towers supporting the lights behind each of the goal lines. Each tower was placed midway between the centre of the goalmouth and the touchline. He calculated that each tower would need to support a light source at least 30 feet above the ground if the beam of light produced was to reach the halfway point of the pitch.

Tasker was working from little knowledge of the lighting of such arenas. Most of the work on illumination at this time was gathered from existing street-lighting systems. Lighting a small area of ground under a single light was a far cry from lighting up an association football pitch.

Having decided upon the location of the light sources, he was then able to place the steam engines needed to drive the electric motors behind the goals. There they would be hidden by the darkness and so would not distract the spectators from the main event, the association football match. To each steam engine he would connect two motors. Newspaper reports of the game described these motors as: "...two of Messers Siemens Brothers dynamo apparatus..."

Each motor would generate energy to power its own Jablochkov candle and each was the equivalent of 8,000 sperm candles. The set-up was repeated at the other end of the pitch. On paper everything was ready, now to put it into practice. For that to happen, however, two sides were needed to play.

It was now that the business side of John Tasker's mind came to the fore. Initially it would seem that a match between two local rivals Sheffield and Hallam would be ideal. Such a match fitted most of the criteria: it was a local derby, the two oldest clubs and not much travel was involved for players and supporters. What could be better? Tasker must have reasoned that he would attract supporters from those clubs, but would he attract the other association football supporters in the city, the neutrals? This was something he was not prepared to take a chance on. He had to come up with some way of ensuring as many supporters of the game were attracted. If only a few hundred turned up, the gas companies would poke great fun at him as would the press. This he had to avoid.

Tasker solved the problem in a very clever way; he would play the game between the best players in the Sheffield Football Association jurisdiction. By ensuring that as many clubs as possible were represented on the pitch, he at least had a good chance of attracting more spectators to the game. So it was that 'The Reds' played 'The Blues'.

The game was to be played on Monday 14 October, 1878. Tasker reasoned that he would be able to set up the electrical equipment over the weekend. Once the game was complete he could then remove everything before the following weekend should the ground be needed for another event. Also the weekend would be a good time to drum up support and enthusiasm for the game because the men of the town would have some leisure time on the Saturday. Around this time most of the factories in Sheffield had taken to finishing work at 12 noon rather than 2.00pm. Equally Tasker reasoned that people's natural curiosity would lead them to the ground on the Sunday, simply to inspect the new electrical equipment. If they did it would be the best possible advertising for the game the following evening. Everything was in place and in

27

October there was still enough evening daylight to allow people to get into place inside the ground to watch the game. There was no British Summer Time in 1878 and the light would start to fade around 6.30pm at this time of year.

He had also sent out invitations to a great number of important people in the city to attend the spectacle and for a few weeks before the game buildings had been erected alongside the ground to house the dignitaries and their spouses whom he hoped would also attend.

Everything was set: the game, the venue, even the two teams had been carefully selected. Local people of importance and standing in the city had been invited. Tasker reasoned that while the men would come simply to enjoy the game, the women would come to marvel at the spectacle. Hopefully their awe and sense of wonder may well rub off on their husbands, whom Tasker hoped to impress. All was ready, nothing had been left to chance, or so Tasker thought.

7. A great occasion

There are always things that cannot be legislated for when putting on a venture of this type for the first time. One factor was the enormous amount of interest the event generated across Sheffield. The other factor was that lighting only the field of play would create problems, not least for the spectators, but more importantly for making payments at the gate. At Sheffield it seems that many who saw the match did not pay an entry fee.

It is difficult to say with any certainty how many people turned up to watch. Even the reporter covering the game was uncertain for he wrote: "We are officially informed that 12,000 people passed the turnstiles, i.e. paid for admission, and that the amount of gate money was £300. It is computed that at least 2,000 proprietors were present in addition. The total of 14,000 however, does not reach the most moderate estimate formed by gentlemen accustomed to the numbering of people in multitudes. Nobody thought there were fewer than 18,000 to 20,000 people present and not a few positively insisted that the attendance was close upon 30,000. So great was the gathering that the mass of people interfered not infrequently with the view of the match."

Officially the attendance was around 14,000 but conservative estimates put it closer to 20,000. To put that number into context, a crowd of 20,000 was approximately four times larger than the gate that had witnessed the FA Cup Final earlier that year.

The other astonishing fact from this report is the number of women who came to see the match. Whether they actually came to see the game of association football or simply to look at the apparatus which made it possible to play the game at night is not clear, but come they did. The reporter also felt that many women had not come to watch the sporting action on the field: "Curiosity conquered the customary courtesy of Bramall Lane and the few who were really interested in the play were obliged to give way to the many who had eyes only for nothing but the new lights. Here and there as ladies came within reach of the rays, they suddenly shot up umbrellas as they would parasols to shield themselves from the sun at mid-day."

It must have been quite a sight that evening for the locals. The electric lighting attracted interest in almost every sphere of local society. The favoured gentry arrived by carriage with the ladies decked out in their finest dresses, bustles rustling as they trailed along behind their owners. That combined with the rustle of taffeta as they made their way into the enclosure and along to the booths provided for the occasion, would have been alien to the ears of the genuine association football supporter not used to such sounds. The gentlemen too; in their finest hats, gloves and canes to the fore would have been an unusual sight at a sporting event.

That sight must have contrasted sharply with the working class fans who arrived in their clothes of rough material, flat caps, and mufflers swathed around their necks to keep out the cold night air. It was an occasion of some grandeur and the evidence suggests that excursions using wagonettes had been arranged from all around the Sheffield area and beyond to transport people to Bramall Lane.

Not only then was it a sporting occasion but given the nature of what was being proposed by John Tasker, it was also a social occasion that ranked with the highest levels of the city's social calendar. This was perhaps something not even Tasker could have imagined as he was planning the event.

It also seems that perhaps Tasker had not positioned the four lights correctly, as the reporter pointed out, once again: "Now and again the players raised their hands to their foreheads to 'shade' their eyes and the faces of those in the booths came out clearly under the intense brilliancy of the illumination in that quarter. Indeed it seemed as if the points [the lamps] were too near each other- the finest effect being obtained some five hundred yards beyond the boundaries of the match. Against the dwellings in New Shoreham Street and neighbourhood, the lights shone with peculiar force and seemed more vivid than on the ground itself."

The reporter went on to point out that other adjustments were needed if the system was to be perfected. He wrote that the more delicate dividing of the lights needed to be looked at, particularly to maintain a constant intensity. This was evidence perhaps that the Jablochkov candle was still in need of some perfecting, even in late 1878. The reporter also felt that the lights needed to be toned down so as "not to be so oppressive to the eyes as the limelight does in bringing out the glories of the pantomime." Overall, it must be said, that the impressions created were just what Tasker must have dreamed of. The reporter had no doubts about the lights and the prospects they posed for the future: "Yet, taking account of every objection that could be made, the impression left upon the mind was that the electric light is not only feasible but in a fair way to become the light of the future."

While that single comment would have pleased Tasker more than any other it would have proved infuriating to a couple of spectators watching the match, sitting in one of the booths provided for the local dignitaries. Thomas Roberts was the manager of the local gas company and alongside him was a company director, Harry Hutchenson. They said that the whole event was not a success and lighting of this kind was simply not feasible. But then they probably would say that, wouldn't they?

The reporter pointed out, quite fairly, that not all of those present deemed the lighting of the football match a success. He did though qualify that by saying that supporters' comments about not being able to see the game as it was played in his opinion had little or nothing to do with the lights. It had more to do with the vastness of the crowd attending the game. He also seemed to have little time for the people who were complaining, writing: "It would puzzle Edison himself to enable one man to see through another's back; and the electric light failed last evening to make transparencies of the more fortunate people who had secured places to the front. The crowd prevented the play being seen by many people who will be disposed to debit their disappointment to the new lights."

Maybe then as now it is impossible to please all of the people. On the whole the event seems to have been judged a great success. The accounts above were given by a news reporter for the paper, simply reporting on the event itself. Also at the game was the paper's local association football reporter and his account of the game itself was also attached to the original article. This itself proves very interesting simply because of the insight it provides today of the way in which the game of association football was played around 129 years ago.

"The match was arranged between the best players of the Sheffield association, the sides being distinguished by the appellation of the 'reds' and the 'blues' and captained respectively by Mr J. C. Clegg and Mr W. E. Clegg.

The captain of the blues having won the toss J. C. Clegg kicked off at half past seven o' clock. The weather was particularly favourable there being scarcely a breath of wind to disturb the light. Though the moon shone out brilliantly, her light was completely overpowered by the illumination. Unfortunately it was soon discovered that the lights were too close to the players, the best light falling on the houses in Bramall Lane.

The players appeared to have no difficulty whatsoever, and had it been brilliant sunshine the play on the whole could not have been much better. This remark, however, does not stand good so far as the reporters were concerned, as they had very great difficulty in distinguishing the several players, except when close to the booths. To describe individual play on the far side was simply an impossibility and the following account of the match is as minute as was possible under the circumstances. The first notable kicks were made by Malpas and T. Buttery, and both did some useful returns.

The blue goal was first endangered by Hunter, but Lawson was equal to the emergency. The reds' captain next had a corner kick. The direction was right, but he had too much steam in sending the ball beyond the goal. Woodcock was next to show prominently, and made a dashing run up the middle, near to his opponents' goal.

E. Buttery next had a corner kick, which went directly to the mark, but the ball was cleverly headed out by the backs. The reds' goal when in imminent peril was relieved at a most critical moment by its custodian. Mosforth then made a raid into his opponents' lines, and just as he got dangerous was checked by W. H. Stacey, who made a telling return. A like attempt by Woodcock was similarly frustrated by him when close to the goal.

A fine flying return by W. E. Clegg was followed by a clever run and crossing by Hunter. The blues once more bore down en mass on the reds goal, which had another marvellous escape. After some more telling kicks by W. E. Clegg, Mosforth carried the ball along the far side, only to be thwarted before getting particularly close up. His next attempt was more successful, as he got within range, but sent the ball outside. Hunter then had a corner kick but without result. Woodcock again proved very troublesome, but Gregory nipped his further progress in the bud. A brilliant run was next made by Bishop who had a shot, which was cleverly nullified by Stacey. The immense crowd could now no longer be compressed within the stipulated limits, and they rushed in on all sides close to the lines marked out for the players, and play was stopped until they got settled.

A corner kick by Patterson initiated a terrific struggle close in to the reds' citadel, but Stacey by great exertion managed to breast the ball back twice in quick succession, for which he was loudly applauded. A determined attempt was then made by several reds on their rivals' goal, and just as their efforts were on the point of fruition they were frustrated by Gregory. Another corner by Patterson had no useful result, but directly after the blues again charged desperately, and success crowned their efforts at 7.50pm Tomlinson making the final kick. The next notable play was some more strong kicking by W. E. Clegg and a neat run by Mosforth. A very effective stop by Gregory - at a critical moment - prevented the reds from equalising matters. A good run by Tomlinson was the last noteworthy item before the call of half-time.

On resuming after changing ends, Woodcock again distinguished himself, and he followed up a clever run by a well aimed shot at goal, but its custodian was on the alert and put the ball away dexterously with his hands. By unselfish crossing by Mosforth and Stratford the ball was got well up to the blues' goal, only to be as quickly returned, when Woodcock again got on the ball and ultimately left it in charge of Anthony, who made a well directed shot, but the backs proved stubborn and kept him at bay.

Hunter made but indifferent use of a corner kick, the ball going wide. Twice was the reds goal in jeopardy, Malpas shooting the ball outside, and a straight one from E. Barber being opportunely stopped by Stacey. A well aimed corner kick by Malpas went dangerously near the goal. More sound returns by Buttery and Hind were followed by a grand shot by Patterson but he was again foiled by Stacey. J. C. Clegg next showed to advantage on the far side, but Houseley landed the ball into the centre. Some pretty crossing by Patterson and Anthony was supplemented by a shot by Mosforth, but the ball went too high. For a considerable time play was both even and fast on both sides, Bishop, Anthony and E. Barber all playing excellently. Eventually after being again hard pressed, and after a gallant defence the blues drove their opponents before them and took the ball through a scrimmage at 8.30pm. Immediately afterwards they again pressed Stacey very hard, but he defended his charge obstinately, and saved it from capture with marvellous dexterity. After another neat run by Bishop, time was called, the blues ultimately winning a particularly well fought contest by two goals to none.

Individually, the play of both sides was particularly good, but the blues excelled as a combined body. The match was in every sense a success though, with further experience of the light will be better concentrated within the prescribed limits of play.
The players on each side:-
REDS: F. Stacey (goal), J. Hunter, E. Buttery, F. Hind (backs), J. C. Clegg (captain), W. Mosforth, A. Woodcock, C. L. Stratford, H. E. Barber and G. Anthony (forwards). W. S. Skinner (umpire)
BLUES: T. Lawson (goal), W. E. Clegg (captain), R. Gregory, J. Buttery, W. H. Stacey (backs), G. B. Marples, J. Tomlinson, E. Barber, P. Patterson and T. Bishop (forwards). R. W. Dickinson (umpire)."
W. P. Bix (referee.)

Match report from *The Sheffield Daily Telegraph* Tuesday 15 October 1878

At this time the Sheffield association still tended to play to their own variation of the rules. For example, they allowed a player to handle the ball to stop the ball in flight and then kick it, once on the ground. They did in fact decide later in that year to adopt the 'London' rules that forbade handling of the ball by anyone other than the goalkeeper.

The other interesting feature is that on the evidence of the team sheet it seems that the teams played with only 10 men. However, it is fairly certain that the two people listed as umpires played as well as umpiring. In those days both sides had to agree to any decision made on the field by the referee and what probably happened here was that one player from each side was designated to discuss contentious decisions with the referee.

So according to the newspaper reports the evening was an unprecedented success. It is better to have too much light than too little, but perhaps it could have been better reflected, yet how was John Tasker to know that? He had never done anything like this before. Also it was soon discovered that it was not enough just to light up the playing pitch, it was also necessary to light the turnstiles and approaches to ensure only paying customers got to see the game.

While all seems to have gone well inside Bramall Lane the same cannot be said for outside the ground. While the game was in progress an incident occurred which was reported in the *Sheffield Evening Star and Daily Times*, the next day. It was headlined: "Serious accident in Bramall Lane." The article read:

"A serious accident by which four persons were more or less injured occurred in Bramall Lane last night. A football match by electric light was taking place on the Bramall grounds and a large concourse of people collected in the lane. About eight o' clock a young man named George Collis, son of Mr George Collis 'bus proprietor', Broomhill, drove through the crowd with a pair of horses attached to a wagonette. He did not stop, it is alleged, to let the crowd get out of the way, and the consequence was four persons were knocked down and injured. One of them a man named Barnabas Ardron living at 11 Woodhouse Lane was trampled upon by one of the horses and was severely cut about the head. The accident was witnessed by Police Sergeant Martin and several Constables, who considered it was the driver's duty to pull up to give the people time to get out of the way."

Apart from that one incident the whole event seems to have passed off to everyone's satisfaction, even the local constabulary. There were no arrests for drunkenness or violence, in fact it was a quiet night on the whole given the size of the gathering.

What would have pleased Tasker more than anything was the reaction of the national press; they like the local newspapers seemed very impressed with the experiment. *The Daily Telegraph* wrote on the morning after the match:

"There was much interest in all quarters as to the success or failure of the experiment. So great was the gathering that the mass of people interfered not infrequently with the view of the match."

Sheffield FC around the time of the first floodlit match.
(Courtesy Sheffield FC)

Despite a few problems caused by the varying intensity of the light, the *Telegraph* concluded that the general impression made on the multitude was decidedly favourable, dryly observing that "those who found fault with the new technology and said they could see nothing simply had their view obscured by the unprecedented crowds."

Such comments would not have gone down well with the two representatives from the local gas company who were at the game; it was the last thing they would want to see printed in a national newspaper.

When all the excitement surrounding the event had died down a little, and calmer heads were applied to evaluating proceedings, the consensus remained unchanged. Everyone felt it a great success, both for the scientific magic that was electricity and also for the good folk of Sheffield. The *Sheffield and Rotherham Independent* on Thursday 17 October carried a reprint of an article published earlier in the London-based *Daily Telegraph*. In the article the unnamed reporter waxed lyrical about the whole event:

"Invention and improvements nowadays tread so quickly upon the heels of each other that timid people may well be pardoned if they become doubtful and anxious.

No sooner do we hear that Mr. Edison has succeeded in dividing the electric light and that another gentleman has given his name to the Jablochkov 'candle' than a report comes that football has been played in Sheffield at eventide, not by the aid of a ball covered with phosphoric oil as our forefathers though might some day be managed, but by turning the night into noon, and making such a blaze by means of four 'points' and a couple of steam engines that the ladies were obliged to put up their parasols and the players shade their eyes. It is too soon to ask where is all this going to end, when we learn that even the moon, which shone brilliantly was 'completely' overpowered by the illumination... The good folk of Sheffield... are prepared to accept and make the best use of everything which science provides; and as the new electric light with its wonderful powers comes before them, they utilise it for the sturdy game which Englishmen love so well."

John Tasker and the Siemens Company who had made the electric motors must have been delighted. They were in competition with the Gramme Company and had stolen a march on them by their success in Sheffield. The 20,000 to 30,000 people present at the match must have been a smack in the eye to the gas companies as most of those attending were very impressed with what they saw. Certainly Tasker must have been suitably pleased with the night as he was to carry on the pioneering work with this new form of energy in the city of Sheffield.

To a large extent everyone was lulled into a false sense of security by the success of the venture. The weather had been extremely kind on that Monday evening. There was little or no wind to upset the lighting system. Equally there was no rain to play havoc with the electrical wiring and equipment. Other companies who staged other similar events at venues up and down the country were not so lucky. For the time being Tasker was able to bask in the glory heaped upon him, his company and the electrical lighting system on display that night.

All seemed to be going well for the fledgling electricity companies and their plans to invade the fortress which was the gas companies. The gas company stranglehold on illumination seemed to be coming under severe and sustained threat. However, there were, sadly, more troubled times ahead for the electricity companies, they were not always going to have the success Tasker enjoyed with his floodlit venture. Not all were using the Siemens dynamo and coupling it with the more recently developed Jablochkov candle. More importantly some had ventures planned for far deeper into the winter months, when the weather was not going to be so kind to them. Some companies were lucky - very lucky - others were not.

8. Floodlit rugby

It seems somewhat odd that given the coverage for the first floodlit association football match, the first rugby match played under lights was a much lower key affair. It did not attract the newspaper coverage that the association football match at Bramall Lane had achieved. This is a little surprising given that it was taking place in Salford, near Manchester, a strong area for sport.

There could have been a number of reasons for this. First it followed very quickly on the heels of the Sheffield game, and second perhaps it was not as well publicised in the local area. Third it could be that local rugby fans were not interested in an exhibition match. Or perhaps it was simply that the club involved was seen as being somewhat elitist within the local rugby fraternity. Certainly from its inception, the host club, Broughton, had been considered as such.

There can be little doubt that the senior clubs in Lancashire were not really interested in or enthusiastic about the experimental new lighting system under which rugby could be played. The county of Lancashire at that time did not have a governing body. The Rugby Union - as was their way in such situations - designated a number of the more well-established clubs within a county to take responsibility for the running of the sport there. They had decreed that all matters pertaining to rugby football in Lancashire were to be controlled by the Manchester Football Club and their counterparts in the Liverpool club. This effectively meant that any innovation within the game needed the support of those two clubs if it was to be successful. Probably they would have seen the innovation of floodlit rugby as being a little garish, given the elitist nature of those two clubs.

The irony is that the very reason the match eventually went ahead was probably due to the fact that while not a big club, Broughton did consider themselves to be somewhat elitist regarding playing membership and saw the event as a way of increasing their standing within the county. It was probably because they were of a similar persuasion to the Liverpool and Manchester clubs that they managed to sway them into sanctioning the event.

The more working-class oriented senior clubs in the area were also not really interested either, but for a different reason. They were run by hard-nosed businessmen in the main, concerned with the finances of such matters. They must have quickly realised that as a novelty, such a game may well attract a crowd, but how big was anyone's guess. It was difficult to see such matches becoming a regular feature in any club's fixture list, given the problems caused to the working man in playing matches at that time. How would any club recoup the expenses laid out in providing lighting in the middle of the night?

That being the case it fell to the clubs in the second echelon, those who were trying to make inroads into what was already a well-established and elitist-dominated fixture list for the senior clubs? Clubs such as Broughton, who certainly were not newcomers, but had not attained the status within the game they felt they should have, and Chorley, who had only been in existence for a short time, were much more receptive to the new venture. They saw the floodlit match as a means of bringing their club to the forefront of Lancashire rugby. They were not equipped to attract the heavyweight media coverage that the established clubs had at their disposal, so how could they counter this?

Broughton and Chorley saw a way round this impasse. They would simply pay a more senior club to oppose them in this evening fixture when it could be arranged. In both cases the clubs selected the Swinton club as suitable opposition. The Swinton committee were hardnosed, but certainly not stupid. They were quite happy to turn up and play a game at any time, provided of course they were guaranteed generous expenses for doing so.

Broughton had begun life in 1869, being formed by former public school pupils, and fed by former pupils of Broughton Grammar School. It was for this reason they were looked upon as a somewhat elitist club, with a 'closed' membership rather than an 'open' one. Consequently they never gained the spectator support of other clubs in the area who were based in more working class areas of the city. In the beginning they were named Broughton Wasps and played matches at the Yew Street Ground. As was often the case in those days they were an offshoot of a cricket club, in this case the Broughton Cricket Club whose ground they shared.

Locally, however, they were never referred to as 'The Wasps' but always as 'The Griffins', simply because their headquarters was the Griffin Inn close to the ground.

Things were ticking over in a reasonable manner for the club in those early years until in the 1877-78 season a new club appeared on the scene. This club also used the name 'Broughton', had been formed a year before by Robert Seddon and only played a few matches. He was to gain fame in his own right 10 years later when, as vice-captain of the 1888 unofficial tour to Australia, he was to lose his life in a boating accident on a river in the Hunter Valley, north of Sydney.

This new Broughton club was known locally as 'Mrs Boardman's Boys'. This was because they made their headquarters and had changing rooms at the Bridge Inn whose landlady was Isabella Boardman. This club played its early matches at Peel Park on Walness Lane.

The first season that both clubs were operating caused a considerable amount of confusion as Broughton Wasps over the years had tended to drop the 'Wasps' from their name while they played at Yew Street, while the other Broughton club played at Peel Park. Perhaps this was another reason why Broughton decided to attempt to stage the floodlit match, to show that it was they who were the senior club in the Broughton area. What is known is that at the end of that 1877-78 season the two clubs came together to sort out their differences and attempt to end the confusion. Broughton Wasps, the senior of the two clubs, dropped the 'Wasps' part of their name officially and agreed to play simply as Broughton. The fledgling club formed by Seddon added the title 'Rangers' to their name and became Broughton Rangers.

Given the nature of the membership of the Broughton club, there is little doubt that they would have carried a great deal of weight and influence once they decided to approach Parker & Bury Ltd. This was a newly formed electrical company in Manchester and was approached with a view to staging a floodlit rugby match. It is possible it was the company which approached the club who they perhaps thought would be receptive to this venture.

What is certain is that Broughton arranged to play a game under floodlights on Tuesday 22 October 1878, just eight days after the association football match in Sheffield. This must really have stuck in the throats of the Chorley committee men who were also desperate to have the honour of being the first to stage such a match. Chorley had even approached the same electrical company but had to settle for a date two days later. There is no doubt Parker & Bury would have felt the Broughton club offered more to them than Chorley. It was closer to the city of Manchester and their club members certainly more influential in the city than the Chorley members.

Swinton, who were to be the opponents in both of the proposed matches were by this time classed as a well established club, having been formed way back in 1866, even before the original Broughton club. Like many before them they had come into being as a result of the efforts of the members of a Church cricket club, St Peter's. Their original name was Swinton and Pendlebury Football Club. When, in 1871, the Rugby Football Union had been formed, Swinton had been one of the clubs in the north that had joined the new governing body for the sport. Their headquarters were at the White Lion Pub, hence their nickname of 'The Lions', one that continues to this day. By 1874 they were playing their games on an enclosed ground on what is now Pendlebury Park.

Given their support and the quality of their fixture list they were a major club in the area and just the draw that Broughton needed to attract the attention of the spectators and hopefully the newspapers. Equally, they were just the attraction that Parker & Bury would want to see involved in the venture. However, then, as now, things tend to change very rapidly. Lessons were learned very quickly in these early pioneering days and Parker & Bury were no different. They quickly absorbed the lessons from the Sheffield match at Bramall Lane, just eight days earlier.

Either Parker & Bury or the Broughton Club took on board the lesson from John Tasker in Sheffield. They decided to market the match not as an inter-club fixture, but as something far grander. The match was to be between Mr A. T. Bowman's XV and Mr W. Longshaw's XV. The intention was to create the impression that these two sides were in fact invitation sides. To the public that meant perhaps players from other clubs would be playing, although this was not the case. The team representing Bowman was in essence Broughton, while Longshaw's squad was really Swinton. Things like today's Trades Description Act held no sway when it came to marketing rugby football in 1878. There could well be another explanation for this ploy, perhaps they needed to use such deception in order to satisfy the demands made by the controlling Manchester and Liverpool clubs in order to allow the match to go ahead.

It is believed that the first ever rugby match to be played at night by floodlights was between Broughton and Swinton. This may not be the case. There were references in the press at the time to other 'illuminated matches' being played earlier, but research has failed to throw up any evidence to support these claims.

It is possible with hindsight to suggest that the press and the club tended to exaggerate the actual attendance. That happened then and still happens on occasions now. There is no doubt that Broughton fell into the same trap that Sheffield FC did and everyone else who staged similar matches around this time. They all vastly underestimated the size of the crowd that would turn up to witness the spectacle of rugby and illuminated lighting. In the chaos that ensued, maybe it could be excused that people tended to overestimate the actual numbers at the grounds.

However, this match failed to attract anywhere near the same newspaper coverage as did the association football match just over a week earlier. The two local newspapers of the time, *The Salford Weekly News* and *The Salford Chronicle*, both published on the same day, afforded the event around five column inches or so each. Both make interesting reading however, as they take different slants on the proceedings. One concentrated more on the actual lighting arrangements put in to illuminate the game, while the other did at least attempt to describe events that took place on the pitch.

The reporter for the *Chronicle* wrote:

"On Tuesday evening a football match was played at Broughton between the club of the district and Swinton. The ground was illuminated by means of the electric light and the novelty of the proceedings attracted a large number of spectators, it being estimated that not less than 10,000 persons were assembled within the enclosure, besides large numbers in the adjacent streets and houses overlooking the ground. The arrangements for the illumination were under the supervision of Messers Parker & Bury of Market Street, Manchester, and consisted of a portable steam engine and a dynamo-electric machine known as a 'Gramme'.

Differing from previous occasions when this light has been used for the same purpose, but two lamps were erected. [This suggests other matches had been similarly lit in the area earlier. However, research has failed to uncover just when and where these matches were staged.]

This was to be regretted as the light was sadly deficient and the shadows cast exceedingly intense, notwithstanding which the game proceeded merrily and terminated in favour of the home team. The lights were excessively brilliant, enabling anyone to read with ease at a distance of 50 or 60 yards, though the effect on the eyesight was not at all pleasant, owing to its intensity and unsteadiness. The complaints so often seen reported from Paris were confirmed on this occasion, as during the progress of the game one light was extinguished owing to some irregularity of the working of the machinery. The astonishment occasioned by the sudden increase in the illuminating power may well be imagined and the applause which greeted its reappearance testified to its appreciation.

The gas lights in the neighbourhood suffered very severely by the contrast, their appearance being of a decidedly yellow and smoky cast. Still it is not very probable that the electric light, much as it may desire, will supersede gas as a standard illuminating agent for many years, on account of its irregularity of working and excessive cost, the latter question being of great moment to the rate-payers and their municipal representatives at the present time."

In this report little is mentioned about the rugby, or if play was possible under the illumination. He does mention in an indirect way that in Paris arc-lamps used for illumination were in use and regularly tended to fail due to the difficulties of maintaining the gap at a constant distance between the two carbon rods.

What is more intriguing, however, is the reference he makes to the lights being used on previous occasions. There are two possible explanations for this, first that he was referring to the lighting arrangements made in Sheffield for the match eight days before. The other explanation is that there was a rugby match played earlier using floodlights. The latter could be the case, but the Broughton verses Swinton game is usually recognised as the first ever rugby match staged under lights.

Perhaps there is a need now to amend that to the first recorded match played using floodlights. Maybe Parker & Bury did test the lighting equipment before coming to Broughton. Such testing would be sound common, not to say business, sense. So was there a match arranged simply to allow the electrical company to experiment with differing lighting systems?

So there is a mystery, was Broughton the first club to stage a floodlit game or not? An even simpler and perhaps more plausible explanation could be that the reporter was just reporting hearsay, gossip, or match-day rumour, and no such match every occurred.

There is one other interesting comment made by this reporter and it is the comparison he makes between gas and electric lighting. It was the sort of comparison the electrical companies welcomed, while the gas companies would have been dismayed by it. The favourable comparison between the two differing light sources would have been noticed by all those present inside and outside the ground. The reporter and the gas companies were not to know, as were Parker & Bury, that the technology of the electric light was moving on at a great pace even as the report was written.

Within a few short years the light bulb would become reliable enough to allow its safe and affordable use in houses, shops and streets throughout the land. Finally the one other point of note gleaned from the report is the interest the game sparked in supporters. Some 10,000 were estimated to be in the ground and thousands more milling around outside on the streets unable to gain admission to the spectacle. This is a similar story to that in Sheffield, albeit on a slightly smaller scale. The electrical companies were getting just the publicity they sought and needed and in larger quantities than even they had dared hope.

In the report from *The Weekly News* there is even more information regarding this event. Their reporter penned the story as he saw it:

"On Tuesday evening a match was played on the ground of the Broughton Football Club by the aid of Gramme's electric light. Probably 8,000 to 10,000 persons were present when the time for kick off arrived. The ground was illuminated by two lights placed at opposite corners, each raised by about 30 feet from the ground. Each of these lights was connected by electric wires with the machines which were close together, and connected with the steam engine. The corners of the ground where the lights stood were, of course as 'light as day', but the other two corners were almost enveloped in darkness, so that four lights ought to have been used.

The night was fine and clear, but the ground was in a very damp state. At 7.45pm. Mr Longshaw's team who were advertised as Swinton kicked off from the pavilion goal, and coming on with a rush, caused the first few scrimmages to be contested in the Broughton team's half of the ground. The latter however, soon forced the ball back and had the best of the game nearly through out until the call of 'no side' when the score stood: Broughton two goals, three tries, three touchdowns; Swinton nil. C. Sawyer kicked one of the goals from the field of play, Mudie the other from a fine try by J. Sawyer, while three unsuccessful tries were obtained by, Riley, A. Bowman and Shutt. It ought to be added that C. and W. Sawyer made some grand runs especially the former. The names of the two teams were as follows.

Broughton: W. Sawyer, W. Morgan (backs); C. Sawyer, A. Mangles, (threequarter-backs); A. Bowman (captain) and C. Riley, (half-backs); J. Sawyer, W. Bell, A. Whalley, R. Mudie, T. Dennett, R.A. Shutt, J. Tomlinson, A. Smith, G. Piper.

Mr Longshaw's team: T. Farr, H. Wood, (backs); H. P. Farn, I. Seville, (threequarter-backs); R. Mills, W. Nicholson, (half-backs); W. Longshaw (captain), T. Barker, A. Hope, W. Evans, J. Barlow, J. Fletcher, F. Wild, J. Glossop, H. Yates."

Given that the two captains were Bowman and Longshaw it is easy to understand why the teams were referred to by those names. That still doesn't deflect from the fact that it was really Broughton and Swinton who took to the field that evening. By not referring to either club by name (even if the press did) in the build-up to the match it was hoped that people would think players from other clubs would be participating as guests on the evening. It seems that while employing the ploy used by John Tasker in Sheffield they went one better and did not see the need to go to the trouble and expense of inviting other players from other clubs to come along and play – they just suggested that's what they were doing.

In this report there is a shift in emphasis, from lighting to rugby. The writer passed no judgement on the illumination system other than to say that four lights should have been used rather than two.

The other interesting fact is his estimate of the attendance at the ground: between 8,000 and 10,000. This suggests the event was a success both on and off the field. There is no indication of the gate money taken on the night, but if it was at sixpence each for entry at least, and if only half paid that would produce a receipt on the night of around £125, a vast sum of money in 1878. On this basis Parker & Bury would have recouped their outlay and there would still have been a considerable amount for the Broughton Club.

The one question that begs to be asked at this point is just why was the coverage at national level so poor? It is true the *Manchester Guardian* did produce a report of the game but that was also small and in a northern-based paper. Was this poor coverage simply due to the fact that it was not the first floodlit sports match? Were the newspapers making little or no distinction between the association code and the handling code? To the newspapers was one floodlit game just the same as another? Such questions cannot be resolved after all this time. What is clear is that from the viewpoint of the fledgling electrical industry the Broughton event was just as successful as the game at Bramall Lane. The media was looking at the floodlighting in a very positive way. Influential people were becoming aware of the possibilities offered by this new energy source. This must have spurred the companies on to increase their activities up and down the country.

The gas companies would still have considered that they were not under threat from electrical illumination. After all they were looking down from their ivory towers and seemed to have the whole situation under control. They were lighting homes, factories, and streets. They must have thought they would continue to do so unimpeded. How wrong they were.

9. Chorley's disaster

The first two sporting events to be floodlit were a success, with the Sheffield association football match being the more successful of the two. However not all such ventures were as fortunate. In the case of the rugby code this was dramatically illustrated as Chorley were to find out to their great embarrassment. It is truly amazing just how much can go wrong in just two short days and at venues not more than 20 miles apart.

In 1878 Chorley was a fledgling club, but was ambitious and wanted a spot at the top table of Lancashire rugby. Their captain at this time was Humphrey Norris Whittle. He was the second son of the very powerful Thomas Whittle, a very influential Chorley businessman and town councillor. The Whittle family owned more than 10 coal mines around the Chorley district at one time or another. Thomas Whittle would go on to become the third Mayor of the town. It is ironic that Thomas Whittle was chairman of the towns' gas committee, yet his sons Humphrey and Leopold, both of whom worked with their father in the family coal business, were about to become involved with a venture aimed at aiding the rival new electrical energy source.

It must have been difficult to reconcile their father into accepting this new venture. Thomas, however, knowing just how headstrong his second son could be, must have taken solace in the fact that the new-fangled invention was never going to catch on and replace gas.

While Humphrey was one driving force at the Chorley club, the other was the club secretary Henry Fleming Hibbert. Henry was an archetypal political animal. He would go on in later life to represent Chorley as its Member of Parliament. Later in 1903 at the age of 53, he would receive a knighthood for his services to the community. While in the House of Commons he was heavily involved with education and in 1919 was further rewarded by being made a baronet and asked to sit in the Upper House.

The Chorley club had already made a decision that in the 1878-79 season to participate in the 'North of England Challenge Cup'. This was a new competition that was to be staged in Blackpool in December 1878. It was set up in response to, and as a challenge to, the very successful Yorkshire Cup held the previous season. The Chorley club however, saw yet another opportunity to put itself on the map. It would also put floodlit rugby on the map, but equally importantly both Humphrey and Henry would do themselves no harm either.

It is unclear if it was they who approached Parker & Bury with a view to staging a floodlit match in Chorley or vice versa. It is more probable to assume that given Humphrey and Henry's business connections in Manchester, they did the approaching. Sadly it must be said neither of them did their research particularly well and were not as thorough as they should have been. They set the date for their match on 24 October, initially unaware that Broughton were to upstage them by two days. It would have been interesting to have been a fly on the wall when the pair of them found out.

They would have done everything in their considerable powers to ensure that it was Chorley and not Broughton who staged the first such match, but they were unsuccessful. There must have been good reason for this for both Humphrey and Henry were strong-willed powerful men used to getting their own way. Yet in spite of this Broughton still beat them to the punch. It seems someone at the Broughton club had even more clout with Parker & Bury. It then simply became a money-making venture for the Chorley club, as the electricity company was providing its services for free. But Humphrey and Henry faced more problems before they would be able to stage what was to become known as 'the game that never was'.

At the time the club played all its home games at Dole Park in the centre of the town on a pitch that was not enclosed. There had been no need previously to enclose the ground, a simple collection from the supporters had been sufficient to aid club funds. The first priority now though was to fence in the ground and the simple grandstand. This would enable them to charge an entry fee to witness the spectacle. They set about the task with their usual enthusiasm, using their not inconsiderable connections in the town and with the town council.

As the 1878-79 season commenced the fence was in place, permission having been obtained from the authorities. As they were anticipating a crowd somewhat larger that that which usually watched them play they realised that having a flat spectator area would be of little use. What was needed was some form of banking that went from the side of the pitch back to the newly erected fence. Thus spectators would have a better view of the game.

Ironically, they approached the local gas works in Chorley and sought permission to buy and take away the cinders that were the by-product of coal after the gas had been extracted. The gas company was only too happy to oblige, glad that someone was relieving them of a large quantity of what was a waste product. Once the cinders were transported to Dole Park they were used to create spectator banking inside the ground.

In the weeks and days leading up to the game Chorley went to great lengths to ensure that no one would sneak in to watch without paying for the privilege. Henry even went so far as to approach the people who lived in the houses that backed onto one side of the ground to seek assurances from the householders that they would not let people walk through their gardens to climb the enclosure fence.

Even that measure was not enough for Henry Hibbert who on learning of some of the problems that had been encountered at Sheffield, 10 days previously, and Broughton, just a couple of days before, took drastic action. He was determined that no one would use the cover of darkness to climb over the fence on the night.

Just how to stop it was the question, and the solution lay in another trip to the local gas works, not for cinders this time, but coal tar - gallons of the stuff. The tar was to be painted on the top of the fence and was intended to discourage freeloaders from gaining entry over the fence. The idea was the tar would not have dried by the day of the game, so anyone attempting to climb the fence would ruin their clothes. Henry should not have bothered. It proved more of a headache than a deterrent.

Parker & Bury used a different system for lighting the playing pitch than that used in Sheffield. That was to be expected as all the companies were experimenting. The company staged both the Broughton and Chorley games using two differing lighting systems. At Broughton it had used only two lights and placed them in opposite corners of the pitch - at Chorley they opted to use six lights. Maybe Parker & Bury was reacting to the lessons they had learned two days before.

The lighting for the Chorley match was provided by two 'A' type Gramme apparatus, each one being placed behind the goalposts at either end of the pitch. Behind the dead-ball line, equally spaced across the field, were three 30 foot high posts on which the lights were fitted. One of the Gramme machines would be used at each end to power the three Jablochkov candles, one on each of the posts across the field. These lights were arranged in series, it being felt that this would reduce their intensity.

However, as the Sheffield encounter had clearly shown, they could afford to do this. By doing so the local newspaper report says that it was felt that each light would produce the equivalent intensity of 600 sperm candles. For the first time there is also some idea of the cost of running such lights. The same reporter noted that each Jablochkov candle cost around 2½d (1p) per hour to run. It must be noted though that 2½d in 1878 would have represented a considerable cost.

Parker & Bury had their work cut out to dismantle the equipment at Broughton and install a new setup at Chorley. As the day of the match arrived they had everything in place; the two Gramme machines, the steam engines needed to drive them, the lights and all the electric cables needed to transport the power. The one thing they had not factored into the equation as Thursday 24 October arrived was the weather. It rained. Indeed it lashed down as the afternoon arrived. And it brought with it problems. The effect of the rain was that, try as they might, the electricians could not get the system to work. No amount of effort could persuade it to do otherwise. The best electrical brains at the ground could not come up with a solution. The cause was easily identified: water. Stop the rain and the problem was solved.

As the day progressed Henry Hibbert had a problem and it was growing hour by hour. It came to a head as the first spectators began to arrive at the ground. In the beginning they arrived in a steady trickle, but then quickly became a stream. Just what should he do? Should he have them remain standing outside the ground waiting to get in to watch a match which may or may not be played?

Humphrey Whittle, as captain of the Chorley team was already down at the club's headquarters, the Rose and Crown in the centre of the town. There in an upstairs room he had greeted his players as they arrived to prepare for the game. They were sitting around or getting changed ready to play. Their opponents, Swinton, fresh from their exploits of two nights before had also arrived. They would have disembarked at Chorley station and been picked up by wagonette and transported to the Rose and Crown. For this match there was no ambiguity, they were turning out as Swinton so everyone was aware who was playing who.

As both teams were settling in and getting changed so the rain continued unabated. Henry Hibbert back at Dole Park had no hesitation, even after being told by the electricians all the problems they faced. He ordered the turnstiles to be opened and then stood back and watched as the money rolled in. He would let the electrical company worry about providing the illumination, his thinking must have been to attempt to claw back some of the money the club had laid out to stage the game.

As the kick-off time approached the rain continued to lash down. The crowd both inside and outside the ground was growing by the minute as more and more people arrived to witness the experiment. As the crowd inside the ground got denser so new arrivals were further and further back from the pitch side. Some seeking shelter from the rain also moved back until people were leaning against the perimeter fence in greater and greater numbers, the fence which still had undried tar running down the inside of it. The results were inevitable - coats were ruined by the tar. However, the crowd by this time was so large and tightly packed they could not move to find anyone to complain to who looked remotely like an official. Also the crowd was now being amused by the antics of the electricians who were trying to dry out the wiring, or cover the dynamo from the rain sufficiently for the system to actually work. The arc-lamps at one end of the ground or the other would suddenly come on. Almost instantly the darkness would be banished. Then just as quickly as the light had appeared it would disappear as the system short circuited yet again. Each time it happened the crowd would roar their appreciation as the light came on and then roar again as it went out.

The organisers of the event badly underestimated the interest the match would generate among the working classes. According to a reporter of the day at least 8,000 turned up to witness this match, perhaps more. This more or less matched the crowd Broughton had entertained two nights previously.

Still the rain came down relentlessly and as kick-off time came and went, Hibbert sent a message to the Rose and Crown that the two teams were to remain in the comfort of the dressing rooms until Parker & Bury managed to get the lights to work. With an estimated 8,000 inside having paid to watch the game and the lights steadfastly refusing to work, Hibbert must have been frantic as to what he should do.

At around 8.30pm, an hour after the scheduled kick-off time, the electricians finally admitted defeat and abandoned their efforts to get the lights working. There were far too many inside the ground to even begin to attempt to refund the entry fee and Hibbert had no intentions of even considering such a move. He contacted the police officers present at the ground and informed them that the game was to be abandoned. Before he did so he had negotiated with Parker & Bury that they would restage the game in two weeks time, again free of charge. All would be allowed to watch that match for free.

At this point Hibbert left matters in the hands of the local constabulary and his underlings inside and outside the ground. They relayed to the crowd the arrangements for the match to be restaged in a fortnight. He stealthily slipped away from the ground, but not before he had picked up the gate receipts. He took away with him more than £150, a considerable sum for the Chorley Club. Hibbert had no intentions of returning even a penny of that sum, so spent the rest of the evening hiding in one of the bedrooms at the Rose and Crown, much to the amusement of the rest of the committee and the players and officials from Swinton.

Back at the ground the crowd was wet, but still in good humour and accepted the situation, realising the difficulties the electricity people were trying to operate under. Most people, after satisfying their curiosity by examining the electric motors and other electrical equipment, quietly dispersed into the rain-soaked night to make their way home. They were content in the knowledge that they would be allowed to watch the restaged match free of charge.

It was inevitable that good luck or more precisely the good weather was not going to last for ever. For the first time the frailties of the new energy source were exposed. It could provide light when the weather was good, but association football and rugby matches took place in the winter, when the weather was inclement.

The rematch, as promised, was staged two weeks later and people were allowed in free of charge. Sadly Swinton, for whatever reason, probably because having been paid expenses once were not prepared to turn up again for no money, were unable to fulfil the fixture on that night. So, rather as Sheffield had done, Chorley arranged a team to oppose them from the best local players in the district.

Chorley took the liberty of actually painting the ball white so as to make it more visible in the game but the match was not a success. The match reporter wrote that on one occasion the crowd was in fits of laughter as both teams were locked in a desperate struggle in a scrimmage to win the ball. However, the ball was in the hands of a spectator standing on the touchline. The light was so poor in the centre of the field that the players had not realised the ball was missing.

So it was that the dreams of Henry Hibbert and Humphrey Norris Whittle of staging the first ever floodlit game of rugby anywhere in the world were thwarted, and not just by a couple of days but, as it turned out, by a couple of weeks. They were the first however to stage the floodlit game that never was.

The Chorley club did have some success that season and did score a first. Even then their triumph was to be blighted by bad weather. The club had entered the grandly titled North of England Challenge Cup Competition, as mentioned earlier. This was the brainchild of John Fish, the manager of The Raikes Hall Gardens, a massive entertainment complex in the centre of Blackpool.

Fish had seen the success a cup competition had enjoyed in Yorkshire. In the red-rose county there was still no official governing authority, that role being filled by the Liverpool and Manchester clubs respectively. He stepped in to fill the void. Being a typical Blackpool entrepreneur he figured that if a county cup competition could generate so much publicity what would an even bigger competition achieve? Hence the title of the competition. He contacted every club north of the River Trent offering them an invitation to play in the cup competition. Sadly his idea failed miserably, only eight clubs entered, and those were all within a 40-mile radius of Blackpool.

Chorley and Rossendale won through to the final that was originally to be played on the last Saturday in December, 1878. Unfortunately the weather took a hand and the country experienced one of the most severe and sustained cold spells ever experienced. Rugby was not possible and it was to be Easter before the competition reached a climax. Chorley won the cup, the only time for which it was competed, but won it in 1879, while the cup, which still exists to this day along with one of the winners' medals, is engraved 1878.

Try as they may neither Whittle or Hibbert could claim to have been involved in the first floodlit rugby match ever to be recorded. What can be said is that they managed to turn that disaster into some sort of triumph on that rainy Thursday evening back in 1878. They kept the gate money and persuaded the electricity company to repeat the experiment for free so honouring their promise made to the spectators.

For Parker & Bury the electrical company, what had turned into a potentially damaging situation when equipment had failed to work seems not to have had a great impact on press or public. The local reporter made no mention or criticism of the arrangements because he, of course, had been unable to see the lights in operation. On the other hand he did have a good story to file regarding the events as they unfolded at a dark and wet Dole Park, so he was happy.

The Chorley game was the first of a number of setbacks electrical companies up and down the country were to endure, along with successes during the following few months. These setbacks did nothing to halt the progress they were making in their desire to become a major force in the country. It seems also that they still saw sport as the way to achieve this.

Left and below:
The Gramme machine.

Bottom left: Zenode Gramme, the Belgian engineer who also produced a dynamo-electric machine.
It was the rivalry between him and Siemens which drove forward the development of the dynamo.

Top: Paul Jablochkov.

Right: The Jablochkov candle. Note how the two carbon rods are kept parallel to each other thus reducing the chances of the arc failing.

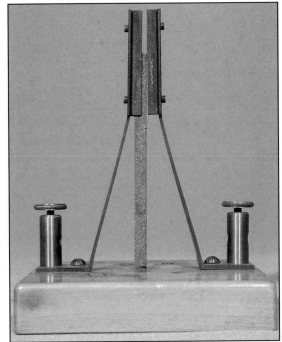

Rugby league at athletics stadiums:

Left: Sheffield Eagles at Don Valley on 26 September 1990 – their first match there against Wakefield Trinity.

Below: London Crusaders at Barnet Copthall Stadium. The floodlights are directed at the track as much as the pitch.

(Photos: Mike Haddon)

10. Floodlit rugby in Yorkshire

It is interesting to note that at much the same time that floodlighting was being used in Lancashire to illuminate rugby matches, Yorkshire rugby was not being left out. But it was in a different county, with a different electricity company, a different lighting system and, it must be said, a different response from both the public and the press to the same game.

Two things are important in the development of floodlit sport at this point. The first is the rapidity of the innovations the various electrical companies employed when lighting games and secondly the way in which counties seemed to stand in one camp or another. The evidence shows that in Lancashire the electrical companies decided to use the electric motor produced by the Gramme company. However, their rivals in the white-rose county backed the machines produce by the Siemens company. Both companies were producing motors of similar capacity and reliability yet it seems even with electric motors the two old sporting rival counties could not agree.

There were a number of matches played in Yorkshire that are important to the development of the floodlit story. These were played in November 1878 and in one instance involved the same club, somewhat in the same manner that Swinton had been involved over the Pennines. The first match is interesting for two reasons: it was the first recorded floodlit match involving a Yorkshire club and a Lancashire club and it was the first floodlit match that had to be abandoned due to a crowd pitch invasion.

The Halifax club had been founded just five years earlier in 1873, but quickly became a force to be reckoned with in Yorkshire rugby. After playing for a couple of seasons on open parkland, in 1876 it began sharing the Hanson Lane ground with the local cricket club. This ground was just opposite Thrum Hall farm, which was to become the club's home for more than 100 years.

The club showed its strength by carrying off the inaugural Yorkshire Cup in 1877. As the 1878-79 season was approaching and the frenzy of floodlit association football and rugby matches were being lauded by the press, the Halifax club faced a dilemma. They were due to play Birch, a club from the rival county across the Pennines. Unfortunately the Saturday the match was due to be contested was also the second day of an autumn race meeting at the Norton Tower course in Halifax. The race course which, incidentally, was the then highest race track in England, being just fewer than 1,200 feet above sea level, was only a mile and a half from the Halifax ground. The committee felt that the clash would seriously affect their crowd for the game with Birch.

Consequently they decided to jump on the floodlighting bandwagon. They persuaded the Birch club to play the match on a Tuesday evening, 2 November 1878. The venture proved to be a very profitable one for the club as the report in the local paper *The Halifax Guardian* clearly showed the following week.

Halifax v Birch (By the Electric Light)

"Encouraged by the success of the Sheffield and other matches, and with a knowledge that football is quite as popular in Halifax as in the cutlery town, the committee of the Halifax Cricket and Football Club determined to arrange for their supporters a match by electric light. Another circumstance, which further pressed them, was that the match with Birch had always been one of the most popular of the home matches, but that this year the date for its decision was also the afternoon of the second day of the Halifax Autumn meeting. It was therefore naturally to be expected that the attendance at one affair would be lessened by the attractions of the other, and vice versa. The idea was then promulgated and eagerly adopted by the committee of holding the football match by the aid of electric light.

The arrangements for the production of the light were placed in the able hands of Messers Blakey Brothers & Emmott, electricians, The Square, and the result of the arrangements was that the coffers of the Halifax club received a handsome addition, and the inhabitants of the town were treated to a view of the light that is to work such a large revolution in the manufacture and sale of gas. At least so the prophets tell us.

Kick off was announced to take place at seven o'clock, and when that hour arrived there was a larger assemblage on the Hanson Lane ground than has ever before been witnessed. The lights were stationed at each end of the field, behind the goal posts and a third on the bottom side. The two former were worked by steam engines supplied by Messers Greenwood of Highroad Well and the latter was worked by battery. The lights acted admirably. More especially the one nearest Gibbit Lane, which was intended to follow the movements of the players, and when they were turned on at the full, at about twenty minutes to eight, the attendance must have been considerably over 20,000.

The Birch team having travelled from Manchester in a saloon carriage, received a hearty welcome on entering the ground, nor was the reception of the home team the less hearty. A considerable time was spent in clearing the ground to be contested over, and even then the breadth was not according to the rule. An arrangement had however been made that the game should not be considered a trial of strength, but that what ever points might be obtained it should be put down on the list of results as "drawn".

Birch lost the toss, and defending the pavilion goal O. Heggs kicked off shortly after 7.45. The kick landed the ball well into the Halifax territory and though the lights at times seemed to dazzle the players, yet the game soon became a fast one. The leather travelled into the Birch '25' and several scrimmages, both loose and packed, took place. From a punt by one of the Birch backs, Rufus Ward obtained a free kick, which G. Thompson had no difficulty in converting into a goal. McFarlane for Birch kicked off and carried the ball into Halifax ground, but the surging mass of people here began to press in and stopped further play.

Strenuous efforts were made to clear a space, but the crowd was stubborn, and so both captains, after having played for about ten minutes, drew their teams off the field, and shortly afterwards left the ground. The people remained for some time, probably thinking that play would be resumed, but they themselves, by their apparent stupidity, had spoilt the game, and the teams not returning meant they gradually dispersed.

Had there been one or two mounted police in attendance the people might have been held back, but beyond this the arrangements were capital, and reflect great credit on the committee and their secretaries. The teams were composed as follows:-

Birch: J. C. Auldjo, W. Pratt (backs); R. MaFarlane, T. Knean, (threequarter-backs); J. Chettwood, L. M. Bell, (half-backs); O. Heggs (captain), T. Hunter, C. H. Kain, M. C. Marr, J. Whitworth, L. Whalley, L. Johnston, R. Simpson, W. Cheetwood, (forwards).
Halifax: John Wood, (back); Rufus A. Ward, J. Dodd, Geo. Scarborough (threequarter-backs); Fred Bedford, Sam Duckitt (half-backs); Geo. Thompson (captain) J. H. Hartley, S. M. Cockin, C. Cooper, F. Wood, J. E. Wood, J. H. Wood, A. Firth, H. Aspinall (forwards).

The gate receipts amounted to upward of £260 but several thousand spectators succeeded in obtaining admission without payment."

There are a number of interesting points in the report. Again, an enormous crowd turned up to witness the spectacle. It was far greater than anyone imagined, and of course the club was unprepared to deal with this. Second, the match was effectively abandoned due to the large crowd invading the field of play.

From a playing point of view the report highlights differences in the style of play of the two clubs. Birch played with two full-backs and two threequarters as opposed to Halifax playing just one full-back and three threequarters. It would be interesting now to see how both sides dealt with that situation.

Finally, the rapid innovation made here at Halifax was the use of a moveable single light so that the beam could be concentrated onto the actual play on the field.

After the abandoned match, the lighting company was again approached to light up another. Two weeks later they were hired by a private company. They were asked to light two matches, both games involving Dewsbury.

The company used a variation on the lighting systems which had been used on the previous three occasions. For the first time, a match was set up and run by a private company, rather than an association football or rugby club.

Dewsbury are still playing in professional rugby league, beginning life as Dewsbury Athletic Football club in October 1875 when Messers Adkin and Heys formed the team. Having set up the club they played their first match in December at Sugar Lane, on a field opposite Crown Flatt. In January 1876 the new club found a permanent home when they arranged to sub-let the field at Crown Flatt from the estate of Lord Saville. They were able to do this thanks to the generosity of William Blackburn. He was the landlord of The Little Saddle pub and loaned the club £15. It was that loan which set the club on its way. Once again there is a link between sport and public houses. The Crown Flatt ground was to be the home of the club until 1991.

As Dewsbury entered its third year of existence, it, like those clubs in Lancashire involved in playing the game at night, was striving to make an impression in the tough world of Yorkshire rugby. Dewsbury also decided that staging a floodlit game was a very good way of raising its profile and putting it on the rugby map. So on Saturday 16 November the club met Kirkstall, from Leeds.

The match was unusual in a number of ways. It was the first recorded match played under floodlights that seems to have been arranged for the sole purpose of making a profit for the people staging it. Those people were the company that owned and ran The Horticultural Gardens, in Leeds. No doubt they recognised the novelty value of such an event and they appear to have organised the whole thing. They contracted the illumination of the ground out to the company based in Halifax that had experience of such matters, and in all probability hired the two combatants who were to play the game.

The newspaper reports are enlightening because they say that the company that lit up the night sky that evening were Messers Blakey Brothers & Emmott. The reporter also says this was not the first time they had done so. He wrote: "...the lighting apparatus was the same as that used in the match played in the previous week in the Cardigan Fields."

Again, research has failed to throw any light on this match. If this match did take place, when it is suggested it did that would have put the date on or around 9 November 1878. There is no evidence of whom the two teams were that participated in the match, or even which code of football was actually played. It does however highlight the problem mentioned earlier, of discovering the first recorded instances of matches being played under floodlights, and accepting that other games may have been played.

It seems that Blakey & Emmott adopted a different approach to that of the Lancashire firm of Parker & Bury, or even that used by John Tasker over in Sheffield only a month earlier. The system they devised, while similar, had one important difference, and showed just how quickly innovation was being introduced by companies floodlighting sporting fixtures. The system used in Leeds, like that used in Halifax, had a moveable light source. True they had a light at each end of the field and were to hedge their bets by powering one with a Siemens dynamo and the other by batteries. Their thinking must have been that the batteries would not fail even if the dynamo did.

Both lights, however, were fitted with reflectors behind them, and one of them had a reflector which was moveable rather than being fixed. This allowed them to direct the light anywhere on the field. It was moved by an operator, who was able to direct the beam of light directly onto the action as it took place, just like a television cameraman following the action on a sports field today. It certainly moved the lighting of rugby matches into a different league. The new system met with favourable approval from the newspaper reporter and a not particularly large crowd who turned up to witness the event. It would be fair to assume that the operator of the moveable light was the same one that had been doing the job in Halifax two weeks earlier. The report said: "... It was impossible with only two lights to throw a clear light over every part of the playing space, but with the apparatus in use the game must be said to have been exceedingly successful. This was in great measure due to the admirable way in which the moveable light was worked, which also enabled the spectators to see the play in any part of the ground..."

It is hard to imagine that the man operating the moving reflector was doing so for the first time, which leads to the speculation that the game referred to as being played a week earlier at Cardigan Field may well have been to test the apparatus and allow the operator to practice following rugby action.

The sad thing is that, unfortunately, the anticipated crowd did not turn up for this game. This is a surprise as in almost every case of these early floodlit ventures the opposite was true. So the owners of the Horticultural Gardens Company decided against staging any further night matches. After all, they were attempting to make money from the venture. From this event it is possible to glean some reasons for the ultimate demise of sports floodlighting in those very early days. The company does not seem to have done its homework very well, as John Tasker had in Sheffield. While they had staged the game between two local clubs and as such produced the local rivalry they wanted; they had underestimated the difficulties of travelling to and from a match on a Saturday evening.

In their defence they were not blessed with good weather on the night leading up to the match. This is shown by the reporter when he wrote that the ground "owing to the recent fall of snow and rain, was in a wretched condition".

For the record the encounter ended with honours even, Kirkstall scoring six touchdowns and one dead ball to Dewsbury's four touchdowns and four dead balls. In those days the only way a match could be won was by kicking a goal and although there were a good many touchdowns no side managed to convert one to win the match.

The innovation of directing the light onto the action was a success as it was in Halifax earlier. It was an innovation that was perhaps a little too far ahead of the existing technology available at the time. However, as in Lancashire, things changed and opinions varied considerably in a short space of time. Nowhere was that more clearly illustrated than in Dewsbury's next floodlit encounter, a week later, when Mirfield visited. Just one week on and the verdict was considerably more damming. On 23 November 1878, Dewsbury were once more in action under floodlights, this time on their own Crown Flatt ground. Once again the system for illuminating the match was provided by Blakey Brothers & Emmott and was identical to that provided in Leeds, with one exception. This time they placed a further light on the halfway line, opposite to the grandstand. Presumably the intention was to light up the centre of the ground so that supporters would feel that the whole of the playing area was being lit.

This time the local reporter was less than enamoured with the whole event. While the newspaper was the same, *The Dewsbury Reporter*, it must be assumed that the reporter was a different one from the man who covered Dewsbury's efforts the previous week at The Horticultural Gardens. The whole tone of the report was much more negative. The reporter's opinions of both the lighting but also the rugby were not favourable. This is clear from the start of his article on 30 November: "The affair was got up by the committee of the Dewsbury Football and Athletic Club, who engaged Messers Blakey Brothers and Emmott, of Halifax, a firm of electrical engineers who are achieving considerable notoriety by the prominence into which they are bringing the new illuminator, by the aid of the Siemens patent machines."

The electricity company would not have been pleased. It was hoping for fame and fortune from the venture, yet was being judged as having notoriety. It does, however, throw up a whole new set of problems, after all if it had become notorious it must have been floodlighting events on somewhat regular basis. We know it was involved at The Horticultural Gardens the previous week and at Halifax two weeks earlier, but that would not constitute a rise in notoriety. So how many events had the firm illuminated? What were they, where were they held, and why are there no newspaper reports? It is puzzling to say the least.

The whole tone of the report follows in a similar vein. It barely touches on the action that took place. The reporter made it clear he was not really interested in matters on the field: "The match was between a team belonging to the local club, and one from that of Mirfield, but it was in no sense a contest, the conditions under which the contestants met being entirely novel, and conducive to what enthusiasts perhaps might call football as one of the fine arts. We will dismiss the players then, at all events for a brief period, to tell of the arrangements for lighting the ground on which they met."

The attendance at this match was considerably more than the previous Saturday. It says in the report that "many thousands" witnessed the game and hundreds of people travelled from Batley, Morley, Heckmondwike, Ossett and many other places. This helped to swell the "many thousands in the crowd from Dewsbury". The crowd did not reach the proportions achieved at Broughton or Chorley in their first failed attempt. It also came nowhere near the estimated 30,000 at the Sheffield game, or the 20,000 at Halifax. At best the Dewsbury crowd was around 5,000, still a considerable number for that club.

The reporter gave a good description of the lighting arrangements adopted at Crown Flatt and they do show that lessons were quickly being learnt. These were not particularly appreciated by the reporter however:

"Passing the pay place, dimly lit by means of naphtha lamps, such as are to be seen on stalls at a winter fair, the crowd of visitors groped their way in the darkness toward the enclosed space within which the match was to be placed. Here and there were 'lanterns dimly burning' but they offered no guidance except in their immediate vicinity... At the south end of the enclosure was a lofty stand, perhaps 15 feet high and on this the initiated told the 'quid nunes' an electric light was to be fixed. Halfway up the enclosure, and opposite the raised benches dignified with the name of a grandstand, was a similar structure, while at the north end was a third... The weather was mild for the time of year, but there was a slight mistiness in the air (in the valley the atmosphere was quite clear) that bit fair to test the penetrative or diffused power of the electric light rather severely."

The rather negative tone of the report continued as the reporter described the effects of the lights once they had been switched on:

"You recognised your friend Jones twenty yards off, and could tell that with his usual good taste he was sporting a green neck tie, and notice your other friend Robinson. Approaching from another direction, was enveloped in an Ulster... You could tell all that, but still Jones and Robinson both looked rather sickly, and it was only when you heard their hearty greetings that you found you were mistaken in supposing that they were suffering from some sudden qualms and came to the conclusion that it was the 'pale cold orb' above which alone was to blame."

It seems that the reporter was more concerned with the effect the lighting had on peoples' appearance and their clothes than on the bigger picture; that the lighting was allowing rugby to be played at night. Once again the ordinary folks of Dewsbury, as in other areas, saw the event more as a social one than a sporting one. A great many women were in attendance, the reporter did not spare them from his acid-dipped pen: "Ladies tripping by suffered likewise [he was referring to the fact that the rosy glow of their cheeks had been toned down and undergone what he described as a sea change, meaning they looked sickly] but the light hues of their feathers and flowers gained in vividness of colour and distinctness."

As if that was not enough he then waxed lyrical by suggesting that a similar lighting effect for the match could have been obtained from a "tropical moon". This begs the question of just how many tropical moons he had actually witnessed to be able to express such an opinion. Equally damming was the view expressed once more that he was not interested in the mysteries of the game being played and was there only to report on the effect or otherwise of the illumination: "Into the mysteries of football we repeat we do not intend to enter, our concern is with the lights."

It is difficult to assess if the writer is doing so with tongue in cheek, or genuinely disliked sport and the new innovation of electric lighting. When he does attempt to describe the action on the field of play he does so in a mocking fashion:

"Muggins has a beautiful chance of seizing the ball, but the electric orb is too much for him, and Simkins takes it. Immediately there is a scurry in pursuit, the watchful electrician on the south stand playing his beam on them. The figures are ghost-like in the light mist, as seen from a distance, and Jorkins as he is on the eve of some wonderful feat, is suddenly lost to sight as if he had dropped down some chasm. Never mind he will turn up in a moment; he has only got into the deep shade which now envelops half of his companions. Half a second and they will all be as prominent as before, the moving beam having been adjusted..."

It seems that the reporter was not enamoured with the electrician who was attempting to train the adjustable reflector onto the action on the field, although he does seem to pay grudging compliments to the system of illumination. However it is difficult at times to pick out such comments: "The engine puffs steadily, the light burns as clear as the sun, and suffers not the slightest diminution in its volume. As for the other lights they too are well maintained and though the first ignited did once go dim for a moment, it was instantly revived, and burned as steadily as the rest."

That comment is a somewhat backhanded compliment to the electrical company, but it is a little difficult to pick out due to the sarcasm that runs through the whole report. He ends the report on yet another sour note when he writes:

"We cease to care for football, and the electric light is beginning to pall, so following the example of many other visitors we wend our way homeward... We venture to predict that many years will elapse before gas is superseded by the electric light. In saying so we do not mean to declare that it is not a great improvement; we are free to confess that it is a wonderful illuminator, but except for open spaces and large halls, there are difficulties to encounter that are not yet surmounted, and one of the chief ones is that, up to the present, the means of producing a pleasant suffusion throughout the atmosphere, in lieu of the fierce glare of a large ball or pencil of light, has not been demonstrated. As an exhibition, that of Saturday was most successful, and that there was an immense amount of light may be gathered from the estimate of the measure of illumination, which we are informed by one of the electricians, was equal to that afforded by 40,000 wax candles. This estimate, we are inclined to think, is somewhat too high."

It is interesting that in this report of a rugby match at no time does the writer mention the score. Dewsbury and Mirfield played a match under floodlights on a relatively mild misty evening in November and not even the final score is given. The reporter covering the event was probably not a sports journalist. He begrudgingly gives this important little detail at the end of the piece when he lets slip that, "the game we are told ended in a draw, slightly in favour of Dewsbury".

The Dewsbury reporter was less than happy with the events at Crown Flatt. His report, if accurate, would suggest that many of the spectators present at the game were of like mind. He suggests that many left before the end of the game, for whatever reasons. The observations he makes are nevertheless very relevant as they highlight a number of factors. Yes there were problems with the lighting systems that existed at the time; although the Jablochkov candle does seem to have given greater reliance to the arc-lamp system as can be seen at Dewsbury where the lights shone consistently.

Second, even by his own grudging admission the event was a success, a match was played and played at night. Third, rapid innovations were introduced in around six weeks or so after a mere handful of games, most of those rugby matches.

There are doubts about that timescale given the evidence, albeit only circumstantial, that other events were staged under the electric lights. But what cannot be disputed is that after the first use of static lighting and six weeks later the companies were using a moveable reflector behind one of the static lights in an attempt to direct the light onto the action as it moved about the field. This was an attempt to ensure that the paying public could see the action. In the Dewsbury match at times the operator was a little slow in following that action but perhaps that is to be expected given the inexperience of the operator. Clubs were also painting the ball white to make it more visible for players and spectators alike.

Crucially, what is also highlighted in the newspaper report is that the novelty factor was beginning to wear off, particularly in the north. Too many matches were being floodlit over too short a period. People were losing interest in such matches and more importantly so to were the newspapers, both at local and national level. Such events were no longer considered to be newsworthy.

The Dewsbury reporter was correct in his assumption that electric lighting would be many years in the future even if his reasoning was way off beam. It was not so many years into the future that the light bulb was improved to such a level as to make it viable for household use. In fact as that match was being staged people such as Swan and Edison were already experimenting with the incandescent lamp. It was that lamp which would revolutionise electric lighting systems and take the electrical companies onto the next level of their development. The companies would be able to take the fight to the gas companies own backyard, so to speak, and move into domestic use for electric lighting.

Hull FC – before and after.

Top: The Boulevard Hull FC versus Wigan, Division One, 22 September 1991. The floodlight stanchions go through the stand roof.

Bottom: The first rugby league match at the KC Stadium, Hull FC versus Halifax Powergen Challenge Cup round 4, 9 February 2003. The floodlights are supplemented by individual lights under the stand roof.
The floodlights at the KC Stadium are 1,200 lux strength, compared to 250 lux at The Boulevard.

(Photos: Mike Haddon)

Bramley versus Hunslet at McLaren Field 1 April 1994. Basic floodlights with two lamps on each pole. (Photo: Mike Haddon)

Dewsbury Rams versus Widnes Vikings 5 September 1999, Northern Ford Premiership play-offs qualifying semi-final. There are six lamps on each pole, with two on the stand roof. (Photo: Mike Haddon)

Top: Widnes versus Whitehaven at Naughton Park, 3 September 1995.
Basic floodlights on poles – before the ground was completely redeveloped.
Bottom: Warrington Wolves versus Wakefield Trinity Wildcats – the last
Super League fixture at Wilderspool, 21 September 2003. Modern
floodlights on the roof of the Brian Bevan stand.
(Photos: Mike Haddon)

11. Floodlights at Newport

It was not just England that was subjected to the floodlit match onslaught. Both Scotland and Wales were also to succumb to the charms of the electricity companies. As the New Year came in, floodlit sport introduced itself to the Principality. It was the rugby code which was to have the honour over its association football rival in hosting the first such event.

As was to be expected it was the rugby hotbed of South Wales that was to have that honour. The club responsible for the first match, however, was not one people would expect. Events did follow a similar trend to that in England in as much as the club involved, Newport, were relative newcomers to the game. They had proved to be successful soon after their inception.

Most rugby union and association football clubs at this time were formed by cricket players wanting to keep fit during the winter. There are however some exceptions to that rule and the Newport Rugby Club was one.

The catalyst for the formation of this club was Thomas Phillips, or, to be even more precise, it was the introduction of a rugby ball made by the now famous James Gilbert company. Phillips was actually from Northampton and worked in the brewing industry. In 1874 he bought The Dock Road Brewery in Newport. Once he began trading with his new company he moved his wife and considerable family down to South Wales to be with him. Two of his children became the instigators of the new club in the area.

His eldest son William along with his younger brother Clifford brought their prized possession to Newport, a rugby ball. It was reputed to be the first ever rugby ball seen in the town and had been bought for them by their father for the considerable sum of 13/6d (67.5p) from the Gilbert company. The ball certainly stimulated a great deal of interest among the young men of Newport for in September 1874 a meeting was called at the Dock Road Brewery, inviting any young men who were interested in forming a football club to attend.

It was at this meeting that the club first saw the light of day. Ironically it was not the rugby code that won the day but rather the association code. Many of the young men who attended that meeting were probably cricketers. They decided that it was association football which best suited their needs. Both William and Clifford became founder members of the new association club.

Sadly, the club seemed destined to flounder right from the outset, for try as they may they could not arrange any fixtures to play association football. The members still wanted to play some form of winter sport, so it was decided to switch to rugby. They had more success and on 5 April 1875, they played their first fixture against Glamorgan Rugby Football Club. Newport Rugby Club was born, and the die was cast. They became a very successful rugby club

They quickly joined forces with the local cricket club to find a field to play on. The cricket and athletic club had a ground on Rodney Parade in the town and it is still the home of the rugby club. So in that respect they did follow the lead of many other clubs by attaching themselves to a cricket club.

Their first full season was 1875-76 season, and they went through that season undefeated, winning eight and drawing three of their fixtures. In those early years the club developed a habit of not losing for they went through the next three seasons also undefeated. There can be few clubs in the history of rugby or association football who can boost such a spectacular start to their history. In 1878-79 they went through the season undefeated without conceding a point of any description, either a try or a goal. They played 15 official matches and won 13, drawing the other two. They also managed to fit in another game as well, an exhibition match against Cardiff. What made this match special was that it was played at night under the new electric lights. This was the first occasion that electric lighting had been seen in Wales.

The match was played on 16 December 1878 in Newport, and demolishes a myth that association football had the honour. It missed out by a couple of months. If this was the first time that electric light had actually been seen in South Wales, the Welsh newspapers seemed not to have made a great thing of it. After the match, on 17 December, the *Western Mail* printed an account of the proceedings that was spartan to say the least. However, it does give quite a lot of information, if one reads between the lines. The report reads:

The Electric Light at Newport

"Newport is indebted to the members of its Cricket, Athletic and Football Club for the opportunity of witnessing the electric light by the aid of which a football match between Cardiff and Newport was played upon the new ground belonging to the latter club on Monday night. The novel spectacle attracted an enormous concourse of people, many thousands paying for admission to the ground, and others occupying free seats and standing places on every coign of vantage that commanded the spectacle. The large grandstand, to which the charge of admission was 1/- [5p], was crowded, all classes of the inhabitants seeming to take an interest in this first appearance of the rival to gas. The ground marked out for the match was 120 yards in length by 75 yards in width and was illuminated by four lights. Three of these were produced by the well known Siemens machines fitted with Serrin candles. The motive power to work these machines was obtained from three eight horse portable engines, which with the necessary fittings were gratuitously supplied by Mr Charles D. Phillips of Newport. The other light was produced by a powerful 50 cell battery, in this case a Serrin candle was also used. Each of the three lights produced by the Siemens machine was calculated to be equal to 1,200 candles whilst that produced by the battery was barely 600.

The Siemens machines were driven at the rate of nearly 1,000 revolutions per minute, and it is a subject of congratulations both to the owners of the machines and to Mr Charles D. Phillips that the whole of the mechanical arrangements although prepared at very short notice worked with the greatest ease and without a single hitch. As to the effect of the lights our powers of description fail us to do it justice. Three of the lights were placed at the end of the ground nearest Newport and the fourth at the opposite extremity.

They were elevated about 12 feet above the ground and fitted with concave reflectors. Each of them made as it were a tube of light through the murky atmosphere and ploughed a broad white illuminated streak on the surface of the ground, from end to end on the enclosure. But for the cross lights reflected by placing the lamps at the extremities of the ground the dark shadows cast by the players and the public would have been exceedingly confusing. When as more than once happened a light did go out these grim fantastic shadows were cast all over the arena.

Altogether the aspect of the scene with its wonderful chiaroscuro, with its dazzling lights and dismal shade was weird in the extreme the only drawback to its picturesqueness being the four glaring balls of light which dazzled the eyes with their painful intensity. How far the light would pierce the darkness if its rays were uninterrupted we cannot say but the more distant light fell upon the old tower by Newport Bridge irradiating the structure so every cranny and mortar joint and even the very laminations of the stones could be distinctly seen.

As for the football match itself, but little can be said of the play of either side. The whole circumstances of the case were adverse to the game of football. The ground was slippery and as hard as a granite pavement. We believe that it was understood amongst the players that the match should be of a purely friendly character and therefore the result that was said to be in favour of Newport, which was only compelled to touchdown once to five times by Cardiff, is scarcely deserving of comment. It is to be hoped that the financial results of the exhibition will be satisfactory as the balance of revenue over expenditure, if any, applied to the funds of the Newport Club; the enterprise of whose members and officials, prominent amongst whom could be mentioned Mr Richard Mullock the Hon. Sec. The town is indebted for this interesting and instructive spectacle."

What was the cost of putting on such a venture in Newport, particularly when it seems the club hired an electricity company from London to supply the illumination? The company was Mr Edward Paterson, Electric Light Engineer of 3 Bedford Court, Covent Garden, London. However, admission to the grandstand was set at one shilling, so the club probably would have more than covered its outlay.

There are a number of other issues raised by the article, not least the lights used. In the north of England companies were favouring the Jablochkov candle as more advanced and reliable than the Serrin candle. The latter used a complicated and cumbersome mechanical system of weights and gear wheels, to attempt to maintain a constant gap between the carbon rods, thus ensuring the lamp did not dim or even fail. The report says that on more than one occasion the lamps actually did fail suggesting that the Serrin candle was the culprit, which is only to be expected, and was why others favoured the Jablochkov system.

The second issue is the use of a battery to power one of the lights. This had not been prominent in the early days in the north but did make sense by using a dynamo system and a battery, the company was not putting all its eggs in one basket. There was also a different lighting configuration, this time with three lamps strung out across one end of the pitch with a solitary lamp stationed at the other end. Also, there were fixed concave reflectors, again differing from the latest trend seen in Yorkshire for one of the reflectors to be moveable. It had seemingly become the norm in Lancashire and Yorkshire for the operator to attempt to follow the action on the pitch by moving the reflector.

There was, however, one fact which mirrored other such events using the new light source: the size of the crowd. While the actual attendance is not given, the reporter did describe it as "an enormous concourse with many thousands paying for admission".

It appears that yet again the event was something of a major social attraction, rather than simply a sporting occasion, and drew many people who would not normally attend a rugby match. So while it was a social success, it perhaps lacked a little something on the playing side, particularly for the purists of the game.

The report shows that it was viewed as a novelty with the rugby being something of an aside. The club's view can be judged by the fact that they played a very important match against Lampeter just three days later. It was a match they won quite easily, after they had played just three days earlier on a cold damp evening under lights on a pitch as hard as concrete.

Many independent reports of matches played under lights in these early days support the view that the lights played tricks, making it very difficult for players to see the ball very well. This fact was exploited on one occasion in the Newport game. The Newport half-back Charles Newman, a former Welsh international, saw that the Cardiff players were concentrating more on the man than on the ball. The reason for that was probably that it was easier to see the man, Newman. On gathering the ball he told his team mate George Rosser to run as hard as he could across the field. As he did so Newman dummied to pass the ball to him - the results were predictable. Rosser made out he was actually carrying the ball as he ran across the pitch being hotly pursued by the Cardiff players. They eventually tackled him and began scrimmaging for the non-existent ball. When they looked up they saw the Newport half-back Newman leaning against the post, the ball sitting on the try line beneath the posts.

Given these sorts of situations it is difficult to take seriously such sporting events from a purist's point of view. Jack Davis's club history describes it as "not much more than a stunt". There can be no doubt the event had done what the electrical company wanted in as much as it had brought to the attention of the South Wales public the possibilities offered by electricity as a rival to gas. The other local newspaper, *The Monmouthshire Merlin and South Wales Advertiser*, carried an even briefer account of proceedings and certainly added nothing to the previous account in the *Western Mail*. It also waited until the final paragraph to mention the actual rugby match itself.

So the whole thing was a bit of a damp squid as far as rugby was concerned, but then sport was only a means to an end for the electricity companies. The Newport club gave little credence to this floodlit fixture and classed it as an exhibition match. It would be a good few years before floodlit rugby would return to the valleys when Cardiff took the plunge a few years later and staged the second match to be floodlit in South Wales.

The rival code was to experience similar apathy from both press and supporters when a couple of months later they staged a couple of games under such lighting.

Floodlit sport in Wales

Top: Rugby: Newport FC in 1878-79
Bottom: The Bee Hotel in Abergele.
In 1879 in a field behind the hotel the first floodlit association football
match in Wales was played.

12. Association football in Wales

It was almost two months before the association game staged a floodlit match in Wales. It is amazing how quickly the attitude of both the media and people had changed to floodlit sport. In October 1878 at Bramall Lane, some 30,000 had flocked to watch the first ever event. Just four short months later a totally different attitude was observed when the first ever floodlit association football match was staged in Wales. It is this different, or perhaps more accurately indifferent attitude, particularly from the media, that causes problems in attempting to research such events. There are a number of mysteries and even inaccuracies associated with the first ever association football match played at night in Wales.

A superficial search into the records of this match reveals the first inaccuracy. Most sources refer to the game being played in December 1879. While the year may well be accurate, the month is not. The truth is that the event was staged almost 10 months earlier, in February 1879. There is also further confusion about the exact date of the match, because two matches were played, a fortnight apart. The picture is cloudier still because both matches involved the same teams.

The third mystery concerns just who was responsible for lighting the event. Again, a superficial search throws up a very famous name, that of Thomas Edison, the famous American inventor. It is suggested by the Rhyl FC website that he was on a tour of North Wales demonstrating "the wonders of electricity". He is then supposed to have hired a threshing machine, steam driven of course, coupled it to his dynamo and proceeded to light up a football pitch to allow two local teams to play in an event witnessed by a couple of hundred spectators, in the middle of December.

The final mystery surrounds just where this first match to be staged in Wales was actually played. A superficial glance is misleading, for it is claimed that it was staged in Rhyl, in North Wales. It was not.

So what did happen? As newspaper coverage is scant it is difficult to piece the full and accurate facts together after all this time. What is not disputed is that the two teams were Rhyl and Grovenor. The latter came and went quite quickly, as was the way in those early days of association football. Not so the Rhyl club, it still plays today.

The Rhyl club was founded around 1875. Its first ground was to the east of the town and it was four years before it moved to Green Field in order to be located more centrally in the town, but it is unclear exactly when the move was made. It must be assumed that the club was at Green Field in February 1879 as this was where the floodlit match was played.

In those early days the team was known as 'The Skull and Crossbones'. They played in a black shirt on which was embroidered a white skull and crossbones, the theory being that the motif would strike terror into the opposition. However, while the Rhyl club would wish to claim the honour of hosting the first ever floodlit match in the principality, sadly they cannot.

The first recorded report of such a match being played was printed in the local newspaper of the time, *The Rhyl Record and Visitor*. It was published on Saturday, 15 February 1879. The report, which is not very long, is quite illuminating. It clears up one myth regarding this match - who provided the lighting. It was not Thomas Edison, but the rather more mundane Messers Walsh & Scott of Manchester. The short report published of the proceedings is printed below:

Football played by the aid of the electric light

"The usually quiet town of Abergele, was very lively on Thursday night last, owing to several influential gentlemen having engaged Messers Walsh and Scott, Manchester, to exhibit the Electric Light, by the aid of which the above game was played. The lamps from which the light was reflected were placed on a pole about six yards from the ground, the wire through which the electricity passed running under the surface, having been connected to a powerful steam engine from which the friction was derived. There were two lamps in operation, one fixed opposite each goal post, and they showed a brilliant light over the whole field, which was behind the Bee Hotel.

A charge of 1/- [5p] was made for admission, a very large number attended, as it was the first time it had been exhibited in this part. The only pity being that the weather had been so unfavourable during the day, making the ground unsuitable for playing, notwithstanding which the teams played with great vigour for about an hour, the game ended in favour of the Skull and Crossbones who succeeded in having three goals against one of the opponents Grovenor.

We have no doubt had the weather not have been so unfavourable a great many more would have come from Rhyl if it was only for curiosity's sake."

All the available evidence suggests that this was the first floodlit association football match to be played in Wales. It was played on Thursday, 13 February 1879. By this time such events were commonplace in Great Britain so it aroused little interest other than a couple of paragraphs in the local newspaper. What the article does clearly show is that Edison was not touring North Wales nor did he provide the dynamos which lit up the field.

So why is there confusion over these events? One explanation could well be that the action then moved along the coast to Rhyl. There two weeks later the two teams met again. *The Rhyl Recorder and Visitor* provided a report on the encounter in their edition dated 1 March 1879. This report is even shorter than the one above but does provide some interesting reading:

Football match by electric light

"On Thursday evening a football match was played in a field in Wellington Road by the aid of the electric light, the competition being between the Grovenor and another club going under the cognomen of the 'Skull and Crossbones' football kickers. Every precaution had been made by the speculators for a rich harvest of gate money by an effectual barricade of the premises; but we believe they were as much disappointed in that respect as we were in the entertainment offered for sixpences and shillings paid for witnessing it. Anything more inconceivably ridiculous we could not possibly imagine than the spectacle of a lot of young men carrying on an evidently purposeless exhibition of one of our best national games. However it was announced to be a drawn game, and there the beribbed guernseys and the Skull and Crossbones ditto rent up a hearty cheer, the glaring light was put out and we joined the disappointed throng in groping our way home determined to apply our sixpence to better use in future."

This reporter was less than enamoured with the whole event. Both the lighting and the football failed to impress him. Perhaps that is why it is such a short and negative account of the whole proceedings. The lack of any factual evidence in the report - and to some extent in the previous one - causes difficulties for historical research. However, it is reasonable to make some assumptions.

It seems likely that the Manchester firm that lit the first match in Abergele would also be responsible for doing the same a fortnight later in Rhyl. Equally it can be assumed that they used the same lighting arrangements. What is interesting is that we are lead to believe that both these matches were the result of action by speculators, rather than by either of the clubs. It is reasonable to assume that neither club would have had the necessary funds nor fan base to undertake such a venture. Therefore both of these matches were money-making ventures by local businessmen.

They used association football as a means of attracting paying customers to part with their hard-earned cash. Nothing new there. As the floodlighting craze reached North Wales the electricity companies were probably no longer providing their services free simply to advertise the new energy source. They no longer needed to; such had been the success of their efforts up and down the land. Now they were hiring out their equipment and expertise and making money in the process. The public was beginning to sit up and take notice of this new energy form.

We can safely assume that the two games, in Abergele and Rhyl, failed to attract sufficient numbers of supporters to part with their cash to make it worthwhile for the speculators to continue with the venture. It was 76 years before floodlit football returned to North Wales. A Rhyl Select played Bolton to open the new floodlights at their ground on 31 October 1955, and almost 11,000 came to watch the great John Charles captain the Rhyl side.

There are references to a match being played even earlier, in December 1878. The two opponents are once again Grovenor and The Skull and Crossbones and there is even mention of a 7-1 result in favour of the Rhyl club.

More intriguing is the continued reference to the name of Thomas Edison. As is often the case, once something is committed to paper, be it right or wrong, as time passes, others see it and use it. A story changes into solid facts. In the Cheshire County League Supporters' Clubs Association publication *The Supporters* in 1951, when discussing the history of the Rhyl club, the author wrote: "It was in Rhyl in December, 1897 that the first floodlit football match was played. Thomas Edison was touring North Wales demonstrating the wonders of electricity, and by using his dynamo and a hired threshing machine for power, hundreds of spectators on a cold winter's night were able to see the town club overwhelm the newly formed Grovenor club 7-1."

The year 1897 in all probability should read 1879, a typographical error. What is confusing is the mention of December rather than February, again perhaps a simple error. Also, there is a scoreline of 7-1 when the reports show scores of 3-1 and 0-0. Was there really a third match played under floodlights in Rhyl? More importantly perhaps, was this game lit by Thomas Edison?

In 1978 J. W. Morris wrote an article in the local Rhyl paper, about the first floodlit match. He also claimed that Edison was involved. The article prompted a number of letters. One, from a Grovenor Davis, corrected Morris on his facts and pointed out that the first ever floodlit game was played in Abergele on 13 February 1879. He quotes a report from the *Liverpool Daily Post* on Tuesday 1 November 1955 on the Rhyl verses Bolton game mentioned

78

earlier. In the report it is claimed that this match was the first in Wales for more than 76 years "since Thomas Edison came to Rhyl with his special lighting equipment for the first ever floodlit match in Britain".

Another letter in response to Morris's article was by Bill Ellis who claimed to have in his possession a handwritten account of a match played in December 1879. According to Ellis this account was written by one of the players who played in the match. This also claims that Edison was in North Wales in December 1879. The writer mentions December and yet in every other respect the details correspond with the match played in Abergele.

He also talks of playing the second match just two days later, yet the evidence clearly show that the games took part two weeks apart. The third contentious issue is the fact that he claims the lamps were constantly failing, yet the reporter makes no mention of this. Finally the writer mentions Thomas Edison as being the provider of the dynamos and hints that he was there. Walsh & Scott provided the lighting, could it be that they actually used an Edison dynamo and that is how this myth has arisen? Yet it hardly seems credible that they would import a dynamo from America when Siemens and Gramme dynamos were readily available in the country.

There is no available evidence to support the notion that Edison was ever in North Wales in December 1879. On 31 December 1879 Edison gave the first public demonstration of his incandescent light bulb. He lit up his factory at Menlo Park in the USA. It is fairly safe to assume that in early December 1879 Edison was safely tucked up in his own bed. It is also established that it was not until 1889 that Edison visited Great Britain. He did so when returning home from a visit to Europe to see the Paris exhibition. Perhaps someone in the distant past misread the date and mistook 1889 for 1879 and so put him at the floodlit match in Wales.

So, all the evidence suggests that the first recorded association football match in Wales was played on 13 February 1879.

The whole enterprise of floodlighting sporting events was rapidly coming to a close, not because it had been unsuccessful, rather it had been too successful. Electrical developments were moving at such a pace they were leaving sport behind. As we shall see later, those developments both in England and America were to accelerate the electrical industry forward at such a speed that it would begin to do just what it set out to do, namely challenge the gas companies in their very heartland: the home.

Top: Leigh's Hilton Park on 12 April 1993. Leigh were one of the first rugby league clubs to have floodlights, combining lights on the stand roof with corner pylons.

Bottom: Farewell to Central Park: Wigan versus St Helens, 5 September 1999. Traditional corner floodlight pylons.

(Photos: Mike Haddon)

13. Scotland lit up

The coverage of the first floodlit association football match in the principality was somewhat sketchy and it would be fair to say that events in Scotland followed a very similar path. There was little newspaper coverage of the first ever rugby match played at night in Scotland. The clubs in Lancashire and Yorkshire were much keener to advertise their wares. Clubs in other areas seemed to adopt the Corinthian attitude of the Rugby Union. To them the game was the important thing rather than the club, so they did not advertise themselves as much as those in Lancashire and Yorkshire.

There is a brief mention of the first floodlit game in Scotland on the RFU website. It says that the first match was at Hawick against Melrose. Hawick won by a goal to nil. There was a crowd of 6,000 and gate receipts of £63. Apparently, because there the people manning the turnstiles were overwhelmed and many supporters entered free.

The match was played in 1879, and fits in with what was happening around the whole of the British Isles at that time, although in Wales while association football led the way, in Scotland it was rugby.

A brochure published to celebrate the 75th anniversary of the Melrose Rugby Football Club in 1952 covers the match. But the club minute book from the time provides more contemporary information.

The match was played on Monday evening 24 February 1879 in severe weather conditions but still attracted a large crowd. A railway company put on a number of special trains to ferry spectators from Melrose and other places to watch the game. Were the spectators travelling to watch the rugby match, or marvel at the new electric lights? The event followed a similar pattern to the first events in England and to some extent in Wales. It was the use of the electric lights which turned what was basically a sports event into a social sporting occasion.

Here, as elsewhere, the organisers grossly underestimated the interest in the match and it is no wonder the electricity companies were delighted with the results of their efforts.

It seems the Melrose club was under-whelmed by the event judging from the entry in the club minutes. It is uninformative, just 16 handwritten lines. Twelve lines were taken up in naming the Melrose players selected to take part. The writer did highlight by underlining (in red) the words "electric light". Nothing was written about the game itself, as if the Melrose club did not consider the fixture to be in any way out of the ordinary.

What is odd is that the local newspaper covering both the Hawick and Melrose areas did not report on the event in any great detail or with any enthusiasm. This mirrors the events in Abergele and Rhyl only a few days before. Why should that be? This was the first floodlit sporting event in the country, that alone should have aroused the interest of the press, but it did not.

There was a report in the local paper two days after the match, but *The Border Advertiser's* article is tucked away inside the newspaper next to the local area news for the district. It vied for space with the likes of the Total Abstinence Society, curling, local election results and other such events. In fairness there is a little more detail in the report than in the North Wales press and that does help form a picture of what took place. The article is short and is worth looking at in its entirety:

Football match by electric light at Hawick

"On Monday evening a match was played between the Hawick and Melrose clubs on the Cricket Green, Hawick, the ground being illuminated by electric light. The weather for some time previously having been stormy and unsettled, fears were entertained that this novel entertainment would not take place. However announcements were issued on Monday to the effect that the ground would be entirely cleared of snow; and in the evening the weather turned out clear and frosty. A special train was run from Selkirk, taking a large number of passengers at Galashields, Melrose, St. Boswells and other intermediate stations. The train took an hour and fifteen minutes on the journey from Galashields to Hawick. On arriving at their destination, the large crowd of excursionists at once made all haste to reach the scene of the fete. Long before reaching the Green the reflection of the light was seen far up in the sky and had the night been darker the effect would have been truly gorgeous.

On drawing near, it was observed that the field was enclosed on every side, and charges of one shilling and sixpence were required for admittance. For a considerable time the gatekeepers stuck to their post, and admitted only those of the vast crowd, fighting and struggling outside, just as they paid tribute. Besides the surging mass on the roadway, a neighbouring eminence was taken advantage of by large numbers. At last the crush became so great that the gatekeepers had to stand calmly by and see hundreds of people rush into the park minus payment. Notwithstanding this, the amount drawn at the gate must have been enormous. It is believed that at least 6,000 people were within the enclosure in the course of the evening.

At 8.30pm the Melrose club had the first kick-off. The Melrose uniform was striped while that of Hawick was dark blue. Each side was cheered lustily as they neared their respective goals. The game lasted 40 minutes and kept up a great spirit throughout. At times as the sides closed in a desperate struggle for the ball, nothing but a phalanx of legs and arms was to be seen. At about nine o' clock the light placed at the north end of the field began to wane, and at that time the chance of Melrose obtaining a victory began to wane also. At 9.10 pm the ball went flying over the Hawick goal, and a tremendous cheer burst from the crowd. The volunteer band struck up a lively tune, and continued to entertain the vast assemblage for some time with a selection of tunes.

The players continued on the ground for some time longer, but more attention was now paid to the electric lights. These were placed at the north and south ends of the field, and revolved so as to illuminate any particular part of it. A good deal of interest was manifested in the apparatus constructed to supply the electric fluid to the reflectors. The two lights were supplied by Siemens' dynamo-electric machines, each light being equal to 1,600 candles. The regulators were Serrin patent and the lights were thrown by two powerful parabolic reflectors. As a general rule satisfaction was expressed at the manner in which the affair was conducted, although not a few expected a more brilliant light.

At 9.30pm the crowd began to disperse and some minutes later the lights went out but with little warning, leaving the field in total darkness. Many people were at this juncture still on the field, and not a few bruised limbs were received as the surging mass moved its way outwards. Thus ended the night's proceedings in Hawick, but the Selkirk train had some additional scenes which were not bargained for at all. The rowdy spirit which prevailed showed that the public houses had been well patronised during the evening. In one carriage a lamp was smashed, and one or two bravadoes climbed outside and hung on while the train was at full speed. In fact, such a pandemonium was enacted that the occupants were dragged out at Galashields, to which place, we are happy to say, but few of them belonged."

Once again, the organisers underestimated the numbers of supporters and onlookers who would turn up to witness the event. This report says that 6,000 were present at Hawick on that evening. For this location, the Scottish Borders and a much sparser population, it was a very impressive attendance.

If that attendance is an accurate reflection then it does question the supposed gate receipts of £63. If everyone actually paid sixpence, then this would equate to an attendance of around 2,500, less than half the crowd at the game.

The second interesting point is that the lighting, once considered too powerful, was now reasonably sufficient to play rugby by. It seems that the companies were fast grasping that the light need not be as bright as it could possibly be made in order to light up a sporting contest. In addition, at Hawick both the lights were attached to moveable reflectors that were then operated by electricians. This allowed both lights to follow the action on the field. In both England and Wales only one light was operated in this manner, the other remaining static. Again innovation was rapidly implemented by the electricity companies. By employing two moveable reflectors to guide the light to all parts of the field they were able to get away with using only the two lights. The slower progress made in rugby allowed this approach without detriment to players or supporters.

This could be one reason why many more rugby matches were lit than association football. That game must have been a nightmare for those operating the reflectors. One huge kick and the ball would disappear and be difficult for the operator to find just as it was for the players and spectators.

What is strange is the actual light source employed by the Scottish company. The two lights were not Jablochkov candles but were based on the older Serrin lamp, which did not provide a constant light.

However, this article was supportive of electricity, although this must be tempered with the knowledge that this was the first event held in Scotland, and the reporter was probably seeing the lighting for the first time, as were the spectators. This can be seen from his reference to the non-existent "electric fluid". The company responsible for the lighting would have been very pleased with the response their efforts received, by those watching and the newspaper reporter.

The railway company was involved in the organisation of this event and provided a special train to transport supporters to and from Hawick on a cold winter Monday night. Judging from the report it would seem there were just as many idiots travelling by train then as today.

The one question it is impossible to answer is a simple one: if this first floodlit game was such a success in Scotland, why was it not repeated elsewhere? In Wales there was a poor attendance at the two association football games. That was not the case here. There are many explanations for this, not least the fact that the season was fast coming to a close, and the game would cease until the following September. Second, games were not played with the regularity and frequency of today so actually finding fixtures to light up would be problematical. Third was the problem of travel - in Scotland that was more of a hindrance than it was in England, although train companies would be willing to put on special trains for special events. But the more floodlit games were played the less special they became.

By the time the 1879-80 season had begun six months later the electricity companies had moved on. Their success in England, Wales and Scotland on the sports fields had given the industry the impetus it needed to tackle bigger challenges. The rapid innovations that were being made in the industry gave the companies the weapons they needed for these new tasks. By far the most potent of these innovations were those involving the incandescent lamp. The Jablochkov candle was a major step forward over the Serrin lamp, but the incandescent lamp was a massive breakthrough. It was simpler, safer, smaller and much more reliable. There were two people making that happen, one in America, the other in England. They would between them make even bigger strides towards producing a better light source. This would eventually lead to the development of a totally reliable light bulb. It was this which really sounded the death knell for floodlit sport for the next 50 years or so. In just a few short months the electricity industry had outgrown the sporting events it had used to launch its products; it was time to move on.

Floodlit rugby league at Odsal.

Left: Wales versus New Zealand – the second match to be played under the Odsal floodlights in 1951.

Centre: Bradford Northern versus Cardiff – at 6.30pm on a January evening in 1952.

Bottom: The 1979 opening of the new floodlights at Odsal.
(Courtesy Bradford Bulls RLFC)

14. Swan's light bulb

In those heady days at the end of 1878, and early in 1879 there was a great deal of activity from promoters, entrepreneurs, clubs and electrical companies, with many floodlit association football and rugby matches being staged up and down the country. Some of these were very successful, others were not. All succeeded in raising the ire of some journalist or another. At the Kennington Oval in the capital, Wanderers played Clapham in an association football match and the considered view was that the lights were inadequate and the shadows produced on the ground were detrimental to spectator viewing. The reports were equally scathing of the practice of having an adjustable reflector behind one of the lights, and the attempts made to direct it onto the ball during play.

That said, the same equipment was used at Richmond Rugby Club's Old Deer Park to light up a contest between Surrey and Middlesex in a rugby county match. All present felt that the experiment was a huge success. Rugby was a sport involving much slower scrimmaging for the ball which must have made the operator's job a great deal simpler, so spectators could follow the game more easily. In association football, a match played at Barnsley got the thumbs down from all the reporters present, who felt that the lighting was inadequate. In Sunderland, however, the event got the approval of all present. Finally when Birmingham played Nottingham Forest the pitch was illuminated by 12 lamps, each fitted atop a 30-feet high pole. Here the lighting was more than adequate for both players and supporters.

The inference that can be drawn from this evidence is simple enough to see. Rugby was, even back then, an easier game to light than was football. Association football was best when a good number of static lights were employed. These lights did the simple job of lighting up permanently the whole of the playing area. Then both players and spectators could see what was happening and shadows did not present too much of a problem. Rugby lent itself better to being illuminated by fewer lights and by directing one or even two lights onto the play by means of moveable reflectors situated behind the lights. And the more practice the operators of the reflectors got the more skilful they became at keeping the play constantly under the beam of light for spectators.

It seems in spite of all these deficiencies, real or imaginary, the whole country was awash with floodlit association football or rugby matches and the numerous electricity companies were employing a vast variety of methods to light up the night sky. Some were more successful than others, but no one seemed to mind. Generally speaking, floodlit matches attracted large crowds of supporters. This was coupled with responses from newspaper reporters that were mainly favourable towards the new electric light.

It was not just the large conurbations that attracted the attention of the electricity companies in their attempts to promote electric lighting. In early 1879 two more rugby matches took place. Taunton played Wellington on a field close to Wellington station, the match being lit by four Siemens dynamos attached to four arc lights. In a return match played this time at Vivary Park just a few days later the same equipment was used but according to reports only three of the four lamps functioned properly.

However, even in these very early stages in the history of electricity and sport, in Taunton we got a glimpse of the lie of the land and the future development the industry would follow. In 1879 Taunton's new Masonic Hall had been completed and was subjected to a dedication ceremony conducted one evening. The Masonic Hall was lit throughout by Siemens dynamos and arc lamps. This was an indicator that the electricity companies were making a subtle shift away from the sporting arenas into both public and private buildings, even in these very early days.

So the question that must be asked is a simple one: after the initial flurry of activity in floodlighting association football and rugby events, why did the innovation die? While the question itself may be a simple one to ask, the answer is considerably more difficult to provide. There are a whole host of reasons for this demise. First there can be no doubt that generally speaking the experiments had been very successful. Matches in both codes had been illuminated successfully, so much so that both players and spectators could enjoy the event. It is that very fact which perhaps was to lead to the death of floodlit sport for the next 50 years or so.

The reports of the events in Sheffield said that as many as 30,000 people turned up to watch the first recorded floodlit association football match. Events staged after that initial match attracted anywhere between 6,000 and upwards of 10,000 supporters. On the whole the vast majority of these supporters were impressed with the new electric lighting. Because such large numbers witnessed these matches, they quickly lost their novelty value. The electricity companies wanted to spread the word regarding the potential of the new power source they were providing, and that certainly happened. Lots of people very quickly became aware of electrical lighting. The electricity companies were more successful in this area than even they dared dream. Why then did they need to continue lighting matches at their own expense? After all fewer and fewer spectators were turning up to watch them. The newspapers quickly lost interest once association football and rugby matches played at night stopped being newsworthy. Rugby and association football had been victims of their own success. It was time for the electricity companies to move on to pastures new.

It is easy to forget that what today would be considered a relatively small crowd was in fact the opposite in the late 1870s. The rugby match played at Hawick in front of a crowd estimated at 6,000 needs to be put in context. It was bigger than that for the FA Cup Final in 1878 at the Kennington Oval. It is easy to think that because crowds of less than 10,000 watched floodlit matches that they were not really successful. But the companies providing the equipment to light these events were highly delighted with the success of the ventures and the numbers turning up to watch.

Other forces were also at work - technical and scientific ones. The electricity companies were quickly able to innovate and learn the new skills involved in lighting up a sports field at night. The moveable reflectors fitted behind arc lamps allowed the skilful operator to follow the ball and keep it lit up at all times. In Scotland that was taken even further when both lamps were fitted with moveable reflectors. The strength of the lighting had been toned down to the required level to allow players to perform without the need to shield their eyes from the glare. This allowed supporters to watch the game in comfort. It was this very speed of innovation in the development of electrical lighting, along with the numerous technical innovations, that was to take the industry away from the sporting arena.

The very reason the sporting venues were first chosen was because the existing technology of the day was best suited to lighting vast areas. This was because of the dangers inherent with arc-lamps themselves. What was needed was a light source that was not only safe and reliable but also long-lasting. The electric arc rods of carbon constantly burned away so had only a short life, if the user was fortunate, of around 90 minutes or so. For this reason they were not really suitable for lighting homes or streets. After all the gas mantle, once lit, would burn brightly for days, even weeks. Light bulbs needed to be made safer and longer lasting if electricity was to be able to challenge the gas industry.

Throughout the 1800s, scientists had strived to create a cost-effective incandescent light source. The problem was that the very high temperatures that were needed to produce light melted most materials available at that time. During the first half of the century most materials that had high melting points were used in an attempt to over come this problem. Ironically it was in 1878, the year of the first floodlit association football and rugby matches, that the breakthrough was made. It was made in England.

Joseph Wilson Swan had made his name not in the electrical industry but rather in photography. He was responsible for the development of both the dry plate and also bromide paper, both of which had revolutionised photography. In 1845, however, he attended a lecture given in Sunderland by James Staite. The focus of the lecture was to show the incandescent qualities of electricity. Staite did this by passing an electric current through a piece of platino-iridium wire which then began to glow. The filament quickly overheated and melted but Swan was hooked.

Swan reasoned that if he could find a material of sufficient resistance to make a filament that would glow but withstand high temperatures he could produce incandescent light. He also felt that if the filament were to be placed in a globe of glass with all the air removed this would increase the quality of the incandescence. He realised that it was the presence of oxygen in the air that was allowing the filament to burn out. It would be 1860 before he was to achieve partial success in his experiments. He placed an arch of carbonised cardboard in a glass globe and passed electricity through the arch. The result was an incandescent light.

It did not burn for very long before the filament broke down, but he had proved his theory correct, the light produced was far greater than anything previously seen.

During the 1870s he continued his experiments and began to overcome his difficulties. In this he was greatly helped by the development of the Sprenger air pump. This pump allowed a good vacuum to be achieved in the glass globes he was using. This in turn led to less oxygen being present and so less chance of the filament burning out.

In 1878 Swan demonstrated the first incandescent light bulb that was of practical use. It had a pure carbon filament enclosed in a glass globe. The glass globe was airtight and a vacuum had been created inside. This new Swan lamp would burn and produce light for - at best - around 13 hours. This was a vast improvement on the 90 minutes or so possible from the best arc-lamps of the day. It also had the vital advantage of being considerably safer to use than the arc lamp. While it still did not burn long enough to be completely practical in use, it did set in motion a series of events that would eventually see the production of a long-lasting light bulb, but not without a legal battle.

Swan had given the first demonstration of his electric light bulb in Newcastle on 18 December 1878 but it had burned out after being lit for just a few minutes. The first practical demonstration was to be to the Literary and Philosophical Society of Newcastle-upon-Tyne on 3 February 1879. There 700 people witnessed the event. Incidentally that meeting had been chaired by Lord

Armstrong who a short time earlier had installed carbon arc-lamps into his house, Cragside, at Rothbury in Northumberland. His was the first house ever to be lit by electricity.

Swan's demonstration was a triumph, and he was even more triumphal a short time later when he installed an electric light into what had previously been a gas lit lamp in Moseley Street outside his factory. It was claimed that Moseley Street became the first street in the world to be lit by electricity. A huge enthusiastic crowd gathered to witness the event.

There is, however, some dispute as to whether it was the first street to be so illuminated. In the middle of October 1879 the premises of the London Stereoscopic Company in Regent Street lit up their shop front using an electric light. The newspapers show in their reports just how the system installed worked:

"In the basement of the building is an Otto silent gas generator, capable of working up to eight horsepower. In order to generate the electric light the engine is worked up to a power of five horsepower, the outlay for which is reckoned at 5d [2p] per hour. This engine drives a shaft at a rate of 750 revolutions per minute, working one of the Siemens dynamo-electric machines, from whence the current is conveyed to the lamp suspended from the facia over the shop front, the lamp being fitted with one of Siemens' automatic regulators, a magnet being brought into play to keep the carbon points at the requisite distance, from each other. The cost of maintaining the light, including the 5d per hour for the five horsepower of the gas generator, is stated to be 7d per hour... The Siemens' lamp requires a renewal of the carbons at the end of three hours... Fresh carbons can be inserted in about three minutes or less."

There are no doubt others who would also claim the honour of being the first to use electricity to light up a street.

On 20 October 1880, Swan once more delivered a lecture to the Literary and Philosophical Society in Newcastle. This time, however, all the gas lights were turned out and the room was lit up by Swan bulbs to allow the lecture to be delivered. It is claimed that this was the first time a public building had been lit by electricity. Given that the Masonic Hall mentioned earlier in Taunton could not really be described as a public building suggests that perhaps Swan's claims had some merit.

In November of the same year he gave a lecture to the Institute of Electrical Engineers. The following year at the Paris exhibition he stole the show with his electric incandescent lighting.

While Swan was patenting his incandescent lamp in Great Britain in 1878, the following year in America the great Thomas Edison was working on a similar design for a carbon filament light bulb. On 12 October 1878 the *New York Herald* printed an article claiming that Edison was already working on an incandescent lamp and had produced a working model of it. The article went on to say that it was Edison's intention to keep his design under wraps, at least until patents in both France and Great Britain were successfully applied for and granted.

In 1879, he did apply for and was granted a patent in the United States. The question was, had Edison devised his light bulb independently of Swan, or had he copied or simply improved upon Swan's invention? Swan claimed that he had first developed the ideas that Edison used in preparing his lamp. This was almost certainly true, but Edison had produced a practical version of the lamp. Swan sued in England, and as part of the settlement of the case, the Edison-Swan United Lighting Company emerged in 1883.

Both the early light bulbs of Swan and Edison used a carbon fibre filament with a cotton thread as the base. By 1880, Edison had moved onto using a bamboo-based carbon filament. The results were dramatic. The new Edison bulb now had a life of not 12 or 13 hours but around 1,200 hours. Now the electricity industry had a light source that even outlasted the gas mantle and the gas industry would be brought under even more pressure from the fast-growing electrical industry. Sport was also going to have to pay the price of this innovation.

15. Decline and revival

So, within 12 months of lighting sporting events at night using floodlights, the companies now had the technology to light up both streets and homes with equal ease. They could do so using safe reliable and long-lasting light bulbs, thanks to the efforts of Swan and Edison. More importantly still, they were in a position to light up factories, mills, homes and the like, cheaply and safely. Owners could light up the workplace and produce their goods 24 hours a day if they so chose, with little risk of the fire inherent with gas. What that meant was that the electricity companies had no further need of rugby or association football events to drive their business forward. They had markets to go into which were potentially more lucrative. So they did what companies do today, they dropped the sports clubs and began to target councils with a view to providing street lighting and illumination in houses.

They targeted business premises which had for years been the sole domain of the gas companies. Electrical entrepreneurs such as John Tasker in Sheffield, who illuminated the first recorded association football match, moved on. Tasker developed the first telephone exchange in the city. Not content with that he eventually became involved in building the first electrical power station in Sheffield. That built, he could start supplying electricity and lighting for the streets of the city and then the houses. Similarly, in 1881, Siemens built the first commercial power generator and used it to light the streets of Godalming in Surrey.

The floodlit rugby and association football matches quickly lost their novelty value and as the experiment had continued with floodlit sport, there was a vast drop in the number of supporters coming to watch the matches. The games were becoming more the focus of attention once more rather than the attraction of seeing electric lights for the first time and were being returned to the working-class sports-loving spectator base of old.

Equally as important was the changing attitude of the newspapers, a vital aspect of the whole publicity machine the electricity industry was attempting to influence at the time. Their attitudes were changing simply because they were as hard-nosed about news then as they are today.

There was another reason for the demise of the floodlit venture, that of travel, or more precisely the method of transport available at the time. For the working man the general mode of transport was to walk or, if they were lucky and could afford it, a short journey by horse-drawn bus or cart. The railway was not all-encompassing in the latter part of the 19th century.

While the trains did run frequently, they tended to do so during the day and, then as now, they ran a summer and winter timetable. Floodlit association football and rugby by their very nature took place in the evenings during the winter months. This was a time when the railway companies greatly reduced the frequency of their trains. The evidence of this comes from the Hawick and Melrose game. The train company there cashed in on the novelty value of the occasion by running special trains to transport a great number of supporters to and from the game.

They would continue to do so only for as long as such events remained special, attracting large numbers of supporters. But they did not remain special for very long. The working classes were used to watching their sport being played on a Saturday afternoon at their home ground. After all it would be around 2pm before they were able to leave their place of work. That gave them enough time to walk to the ground, pay and watch their heroes perform. This was so particularly in the north and those actually playing would have to leave work early thus losing money by doing so. This lost money was then paid to them by the rugby or association football club, and became known as 'broken time' payment.

To ask a working man who was to finish work at around 6pm in the evening to then attempt to travel to a match being played under electric lights that may well kick off at 7.30pm or 8pm was a bit much. They may well put themselves out on the one occasion to witness electric lighting for the first time. They were not going to do so regularly, even if they could afford it. The entrepreneurs in North Wales found out that much to their cost, when they failed to recoup enough from their ventures in Abergele and Rhyl with the Rhyl and Grovenor association football clubs.

The rugby club chairmen, particularly in the north, were realists and knew that a local derby played on a Saturday afternoon would bring a full house every time. A floodlit venture would work once, but certainly no more than that. As the old maxim says: 'If it ain't broke don't fix it'. The clubs tended to stick with what they knew best. They had been happy to go along with the electricity companies to a point. If it did not cost them cash, they were very happy, otherwise it was no deal. In the beginning it had suited the electricity companies to fund these early experiments - now they really had no need to do so, having achieved their aims.

The experiment was a great success, but only in the publicity it gained for the electricity industry and the electric light, not for the association football or rugby clubs. Within a few short months the industry had moved on so far and so fast it left the requirement to use sport behind. It had used association football and rugby for its own ends and if its rapid development was to be sustained and it was to mount a serious challenge to gas it now needed another vehicle. Sport was dispensable and so was dropped. Then as now business came first.

There were still occasional matches, usually rugby games, played under floodlights. In 1888 at Newport's Rodney Parade in South Wales a match was played under lights. It seems that association football was not equally keen to get involved and there were few if any matches played under lights until after the Second World War.

Electricity was now in the minds of the vast majority of the population and they were ready to accept it. The electricity companies could compete with the gas industry on a more level playing field.

As for floodlit sport, it had a somewhat mixed reception over the next 50 years or so. There are references to both association football and rugby matches being played under lights but they were infrequent. In the late 1880s a number of matches were played using Wells lights. These were lamps that pumped oil under pressure into a burner. When lit this created a bright flare. At the beginning of 1889, Wigan and St Helens played such a match lit this way. It was played at Saints' Denton Green Lane ground and attracted a crowd estimated to be 7,000 to watch the action. It was lit using 12 Wells lamps positioned around the ground. St Helens travelled to Halifax in February the same year to take part in a similar experiment. The experiments failed because the light produced was not bright enough to illuminate the games, nor was it very reliable or safe. While the lamps were elevated the oil contained in drums was kept on the ground and these were vulnerable to supporters knocking them over. Because a naked flame was produced it was proved to be unsafe when clubs attempted to use them to illuminate the turnstiles into the grounds and the terraces where the supporters stood.

Further evidence of this safety aspect was experienced by the Swinton club who saw a stand at their Station Road ground reduced to ashes when a Wells light set fire to the wooden structure during a training session. The players were training by the light of the Wells lamp when it ignited the stand with disastrous results. After that the Wells lights fell into disrepute and the experiments came to an end.

It was not until the late 1920s and early 1930s that the use of floodlights in sport began to make a comeback. The launch of greyhound racing in 1926, and the development of speedway, often using the same stadiums, was clearly commercial. Floodlights allowed these sporting entrepreneurs to attract better crowds to their events. Arguably both sports are a better spectacle under lights. By the mid-1930s speedway was attracting vast crowds to venues such as West Ham and Wembley.

In team sports, rugby league led the way. The rugby union and football authorities of the time had banned the use of floodlighting, but the RFL relaxed their ban when an opportunity for regular floodlit matches arose.

Once more an entrepreneur was behind the move to reintroduce the lights, Brigadier General Critchley, who at the time was the owner of the White City Stadium in west London. He managed to convince both the Wigan and Leeds rugby league clubs to travel down to the capital to play a match under floodlights. A crowd of 10,000 turned up to witness the contest and it was enough to convince Critchley that the venture should continue and could succeed.

He took over the struggling Wigan Highfield club, and with the Rugby Football League's agreement moved the team to London, playing home league matches on Wednesday nights under floodlights at White City.

The players remained mainly based in Wigan, and travelled down to London on Wednesday afternoons for home matches, then caught the midnight train home from Euston so they could go to work the next day. Initially, the crowds were good, and the Australian tourists drew 10,541 on 22 November. The first French tourists played at White City on 21 March 1934, 1,922 fans seeing them lose narrowly 19-17. But crowds dropped towards the end of this first season of floodlit rugby in the capital. The club showed a small loss on the first season, and the team moved to Liverpool, playing at Critchley's Stanley Greyhound Stadium.

White City's floodlights had 40 million candle power (although various sources say 25 or 35 million), and the teams came out solely lit by a spotlight, with the stadium lights gradually coming on. But White City had a capacity of around 80,000 – a speedway meeting in 1928 attracted 78,000 – and the crowds for rugby league must have seemed lost in this vast bowl of a stadium.

The Second World War then intervened in the progress of floodlighting matches, but the technology was making progress. After the war it was football and rugby league that took up the baton and reintroduced night-time team sports. In football Arsenal led the way, in rugby league it was Bradford Northern and Leigh, with the Yorkshire club being the first to install floodlighting for rugby league. On 31 October 1951, Bradford Northern entertained the touring New Zealand Kiwis at Odsal Stadium.

It was a bright, clear evening and was not too cold for the time of year. The supporters flocked in their thousands to watch the encounter. Bradford's floodlights being switched on hugely increased the interest. The lights were fixed along the stand roofs, with others on wooden poles around the speedway track. The system had 43 lamps of 1,000 watts each, and cost £2,000.

Then, as now, the Bradford board had a flair for the theatrical and dramatic, and made a superb job of presenting the match to the public. The vast stadium, with a capacity of more than 100,000, was lit with only small lights, which left the field in total darkness. There was enough lighting to enable spectators to get to their seats and places on the terraces, but they were unable to see very much of the field. Unbeknown to the 29,072 who witnessed the game, apart from those supporters by the entrance to the field, both sets of players and the match officials quietly took the field and lined up as per the programme. Once in position and as the kick-off time of 7.30pm approached the floodlights were switched on. The result was breathtaking as the stadium and pitch were bathed in bright light, which banished the darkness of the night, and the whole view suddenly appeared in front of everyone. The result was pure theatre, the pitch looked like a billiard table. The contrasting strips - New Zealand in stark black with a thin white vee, Bradford in all white with a yellow red and black band round their chest - stood out from the green pitch.

Northern won 13-8, but the tourists were so impressed with the whole event, or perhaps with the size of the crowd, that they quickly rearranged their match against Wales. They persuaded the authorities to allow the game to be played at Bradford under the floodlights, which they readily did. However, only 8,568 supporters came to see the Kiwis win 15-3. The attraction of the new floodlights was undermined by snow and rain.

On 12 January 1952 the first league game was played under the Odsal lights: Bradford beat Cardiff 38-5 in front of 16,000 fans. The match kicked off at 6.30pm, presumably to avoid a clash with the live television coverage of Wigan versus Wakefield Trinity earlier that afternoon.

Few other clubs were as enamoured with floodlights as Bradford Northern. Across the Pennines Leigh took up the cudgel and installed lights but the rest saw no reason to shell out such money when they felt there was no need, after all, daylight was free.

One of the interested spectators at the 1932 floodlit rugby league game at White City was Herbert Chapman, the manager of Arsenal FC, who was most impressed by what he saw. There was little he could do as the Football Association had in August 1930 passed a resolution banning competitive matches from being played under such lights.

There seems to be no reason for the FA's decision other than that they did not like change. They passed the following resolution:

"Attention having been called to the fact that the playing of matches under artificial light is being organised the Council express their opinion that the playing of matches under such conditions is undesirable, and that clubs, members of the association, are prohibited from taking part in such games."

The minutes of the Council give no indication of why floodlights were undesirable, the officials just decided that they were.

In December 1932, just two years later they relaxed the ruling temporarily when a resolution was received from a 'Conference of Football League Clubs of London and Watford'. This group was allowed to play a charity match under lights at White City. Just after the war, Liverpool played a match under floodlights while on tour in the USA. Other teams on tour may have also experienced the novelty of floodlit football.

But it was only in 1950 that the FA's position changed. The first competitive match played under lights was on 1 October 1951 when Southampton met Tottenham at The Dell in a Football Combination B match.

Arsenal had already installed floodlights and were staging high-profile friendly matches. A crowd of 44,385 saw the first against Hapoel Tel Aviv in September 1951. Two weeks later, on 8 October, Hendon FC visited Highbury to play Arsenal in the London Challenge Cup and won 1-0. This was the first floodlit cup match.

Floodlighting in association football soon spread. In 1955 Wembley Stadium installed floodlights, and the development of European club competitions made the installation of floodlights essential for the top clubs. By the late 1950s, even some non-league clubs were installing lights. In 1955 the first FA cup tie was played under lights, when Carlisle entertained Darlington. On 22 February 1956 the first floodlit league match was played, Portsmouth playing Newcastle United at Fratton Park.

Having seen the 1932 experiment involving their rival code, rugby league, the RFU had no intention of following rugby league, which they regarded as the 'professional' code. In 1933 the RFU Council passed a resolution banning the use of floodlights at all games under their jurisdiction, claiming that the floodlights were, "detrimental to the game". The minutes of the RFU recorded: "It was decided that football by floodlight when gate money is taken is not in the interests of the game and must be discouraged."

Rugby union club matches in England were not watched by huge crowds in those days so their decision had little or no effect on the game as a whole and it was not until the late 1950s that floodlights appeared. Lights were installed at Crosskeys' Pandy Park ground in South Wales. The installation was done by a local welfare organisation who owned the ground. The first club to install floodlights was Newport. They staged their first match, against an International XV, on 9 October 1957.

One reason that the football authorities had opposed floodlights was that they feared there would be pressure for new competitions. This soon happened in rugby union. In 1964, the Floodlit Alliance was set up in South Wales and South West England, and was the first 'league' competition for the leading senior clubs in this area. Newport and Bristol had to ask the RFU for permission to join, and were refused, because the RFU did not want competition in club rugby. Jack Davis, who covered Newport for the local paper, called the ban "disgracefully hypocritical" and pointed out that there were other competitions in rugby union, including the Border League in Scotland and a league in Ireland. Ebbw Vale had initiated the tournament, and were the victors in the competition staged over two-leg matches which were decided by which team scored most tries.

In England, the first post-war floodlit match was between Harlequins and Cardiff, on 12 October 1954 at White City. Quins used White City between 1954 and 1960 as a home ground if Twickenham was unavailable. Their 8-6 victory was seen by 18,720 supporters, far higher than their usual crowd of around 1,100. Cardiff returned three times in the 1950s for floodlit friendly matches, although the final match on 21 October 1959 was seen by only 2,646 supporters, which showed that the novelty had worn off.

In 1964 floodlights were installed at Leicester RFC's Welford Road ground. But at the RFU's national stadium, Twickenham, the first match under lights was in 1995 when they were used for the Oxford versus Cambridge Varsity match. Remarkably, this was 40 years after they were first used at Wembley Stadium.

It had taken more than 70 years for the experiments carried out by John Tasker to come to fruition. Often the period from the 1930s to the 1950s is regarded as the era of innovation and experimentation with floodlighting for both association football and rugby. Sadly, the work of those pioneering people of the fledgling electricity industry along with some far-sighted association football and rugby club chairmen all those years ago is now forgotten, and the men responsible long gone.

Today supporters assume that sport, particularly football and rugby will always be available on television. History says that this may not be the case. Way back in 1878 sport had its first encounter with big business. It was used and then cast aside when it outlived its usefulness. This could happen once again as the short-lived 1955 Television Trophy and the longer-lived BBC2 Floodlit Trophy Competition show.

The ITV Television Trophy

The Rugby League

TELEVISION TROPHY FINAL

BY scoring a higher margin than any of the other teams competing in the preliminary rounds, Leigh and Warrington qualify to enter the final of the Rugby League TELEVISION TROPHY series.

These games have provided keen, exciting entertainment and unconversant Londoners have quickly become ardent followers.

This London soccer stronghold of ours has seen very little Rugby League football prior to the advent of the TELEVISION TROPHY series and it is no exaggeration to say it has enhanced the sport's popularity "down South."

A word of praise for the tough athletes from the North. In conditions far from ideal, their performances have been of Gargantuan stature, particularly during those first two games at Loftus Road which were played in severe rainstorms.

GORDON BRADLEY

LEIGH v WARRINGTON

(CHERRY AND WHITE JERSEYS)   (WHITE JERSEYS WITH BLUE AND YELLOW STRIPES)

#	Position	Leigh	#	Position	Warrington
1	Full-Back	J. LEDGARD	1	Full-Back	E. FRASER
2	Right Wing Three-Quarter	J. GIBSON	2	Right Wing Three-Quarter	B. BEVAN
3	Centre Three-Quarter	R. WILSON	3	Centre Three-Quarter	L. HORTON
4	Centre Three-Quarter	J. MURPHY	4	Centre Three-Quarter	A. NAUGHTON
5	Left Wing Three-Quarter	K. HOLDEN	5	Left Wing Three-Quarter	W. KIBRIDE
6	Stand-Off-Half	A. MOORE	6	Stand-Off-Half	E. FRODSHAM
7	Scrum-Half	T. O'BRIEN	7	Scrum-Half	G. HELME
8	Field-Side Prop Forward	W. ROBINSON	8	Field-Side Prop Forward	D. NAUGHTON
9	Hooker	M. DICKENS	9	Hooker	T. McKINNEY
10	Prop Forward	S. OWEN	10	Prop Forward	P. O'TOOLE
11	2nd Row	P. DAVIES	11	2nd Row	H. BATH
12	2nd Row	J. CROOK	12	2nd Row	R. RYAN
13	Loose Forward	J. McFARLANE	13	Loose Forward	W. McFARLANE

Referee : MR. R. GELDER

THE BAND OF THE IRISH GUARDS

(By kind permission of COL. P. F. I. REID, O.B.E., Lt.-Col. Commanding The Irish Guards)
Director of Music : CAPT. C. H. JAEGER, MUS. BAC., L.R.A.M., A.R.C.M. p.s.m.

Presentation of Trophy by Mr. JOHN SPENCER WILLS, M.Inst.T., Chairman of Associated Rediffusion.

THE NATIONAL ANTHEM

Top left: The programme cover from the first game. Top right: The programme cover from the final. Bottom: the teams in the programme from the final.

16. The television age

In the 1950s commercial television was the 'new' industry that searched for a vehicle which would attract viewers.

On 22 September 1955 the new Independent Television Authority was launched as a commercial rival to the established BBC. The first franchise was for London only, and one of the ITA companies, Associated-Rediffusion tried to develop its sports coverage. Some clubs tried to set up a British Floodlit football league, with matches live on ITA. The FA supported the idea, but it was blocked by the Football League. However, rugby league was more accommodating, and the Rugby League Television Trophy was launched as a floodlit competition.

In August, the RFL Council had discussed a floodlit competition. The matter had been raised earlier at their June meeting, but now various ideas were considered. One was to stage tournaments at Leigh and Bradford, with clubs being split into two groups, of 16 clubs and 12, and then further divided into four playing pools. The receipts would be split between the clubs and the RFL. Another proposal came after a visit by Bill Fallowfield to Associated-Rediffusion Ltd, who proposed that a competition be staged in the north and in London. The television company was prepared to guarantee £800 for each match in London, arrange for a suitable stadium, and cover any deficit.

The BBC were also interested in a floodlit tournament, but had told the RFL that no equipment to cover outside broadcasts in the north would be available until November. Gordon Bradley from Associated-Rediffusion came to the RFL meeting, and it was agreed to go ahead with the tournament in London.

A five-game format was agreed. Eight teams entered with the two teams with the biggest winning margin making it to the final. The clubs were paid £400 for their efforts, which was quite considerable, although they had to travel down to the London area to play in a midweek game.

Why the clubs had to go to the locality of the television company rather than the other way round is unclear, although it may have been cheaper for the teams to travel to London than transporting the cumbersome broadcasting equipment to the north.

All of the matches were to be played under lights at grounds around London. The matches were scheduled to be played midweek and were only televised in London, which was the only region receiving the new channel. The television transmitter at Winter Hill in Lancashire was still six months away from completion, so there was no way the games could reach the northern rugby league fans.

It does seem strange that the television company would wish to broadcast rugby league, because at that time, the game was hardly played in the south of England. However, sport was clearly important in trying to develop the new commercial channel, and rugby union would not have become involved because of the 'professionalism' implications of the clubs being paid to play - it was clearly a business decision.

The occasional international match and the annual Wembley Challenge Cup Final was, at that time, the only fare on offer for rugby league followers in the capital. There may have been some supporters of the defunct 1930s Acton & Willesden or Streatham & Mitcham clubs, or even London Highfield still around. But filling the stadiums was not a priority, finding live evening sport for the new channel clearly was. The draw produced the following ties:

Huddersfield versus Wigan
Leigh versus Hunslet
Oldham versus Featherstone Rovers
Warrington versus Wakefield

Of the competing teams, Warrington were the current league champions, having beaten Oldham 7-3 in the 1955 final. Wigan and Leigh had finished fifth and sixth in 1954-55, Featherstone ninth, Huddersfield 11th, Hunslet 14th and Wakefield Trinity 16th.

Huddersfield met Wigan at The Woolwich Stadium on 28 September 1955 in the first of the four initial matches, and won 33-11. Crucially the winning margin of 22 points was not enough to take them through to the final.

The television company was not overspending on publicity. The match programme was a simple four page sheet printed in blue on white paper. The cover named the clubs and stated that "This is the first of five games to be played for the Rugby League Television Trophy presented by Associated-Rediffusion." Inside the teams were printed and there was a summary of rugby league rules.

There was limited coverage in the local papers. *The Kentish Mercury* printed a preview of the Huddersfield versus Wigan game in its 23 September edition, which while sparse did provide some very interesting information:

"With the Americans having left the place intact after last Saturday's [American] football game, Woolwich Stadium is taken over next Wednesday by the equally rugged and slightly less padded gentlemen of the Rugby League.

Sponsors, television firm Associated-Rediffusion, have arranged a five-match competition between northern clubs for a trophy, and crack sides Wigan and Huddersfield oppose each other in the first of them. The game is floodlit starting at 8pm with the broadcast lasting from 8.45 - 9.30.

To help provide ITA's cameramen with practice, Westcombe Park RFC transferred their training from their own headquarters to Queen's Park Rangers' ground at Shepherd's Bush on Wednesday night for a practice session under the lights.

The telecast went out on to ITA's closed circuit screens - the first time rugby union has ever been televised under floodlights.

Combe were invited as the guinea pigs by Ken Johnstone, a recent arrival at Petts Wood and now a member of the club. He's responsible for televising sport for ITA and chose his new club for the dummy run."

However, the game was played on a Wednesday night and the paper was published on Fridays, and their printing deadlines may explain why they did not carry a report of the match.

It is not possible to ascertain why Woolwich Stadium was chosen for the match. It was a multi-use stadium where Charlton Athletic staged some junior football matches. It had a capacity of about 10,000.

The competition then moved to Queen's Park Rangers FC's Loftus Road ground in west London, which staged the rest of the matches. The *Shepherd's Bush Gazette* said that the second-half would be shown as part of ITA's *Cavalcade of Sport* programme. The programme organiser, Mr Gordon Bradley told the newspaper that "the idea was to popularise rugby league football – a game that was faster and much more of a spectacle than soccer or rugby union. The television company had a three-year agreement with QPR to use the Loftus Road ground to stage various sports."

Leigh romped home against Hunslet 46-20 in the second televised match, played on 19 October, a 26-point winning margin. Again, the local paper was published on a Wednesday and did not report the match, which took place on the evening of its publication. However, when it previewed the next game, it said that "...A magnificent passing movement by Leigh towards the end of the [previous] game brought the stands to their feet, and a few moments later, when former England player and captain of the Leigh team, Ledgard, converted, the applause, though on a minor scale, was reminiscent of Twickenham at its best."

The *Gazette* said that the third match, between Oldham and Featherstone, continued the 'War of the Roses' in the tournament, and that "the first two games were very well accepted and created

103

a great deal of excitement among spectators present. Oldham managed to beat their Yorkshire rivals, but only by one point, winning 8-7, not enough to take them to the final.

When Warrington beat Wakefield Trinity 33-9 on 9 November, they piped Huddersfield to a final place, by two points, having a 24-point winning margin.

On 16 November 1955 Warrington turned out a full-strength side to contest the final. Leigh, on the other hand, even though they had played their first round match over a month previously, turned out a weakened side, missing seven first team regulars. The encounter drew a crowd of around 3,500, although the television viewing figures are unknown.

The *Gazette* said that "The series... has aroused a great deal of interest among sporting enthusiasts down south... These matches... have been gaining popular support each week and this faster and more open form of rugby football has caught the imagination of midweek sporting fans." Tickets were priced at 5 shillings (25p), 3 shillings (15p) and 2 shillings (10p). An additional attraction was that the Band of Her Majesty's Irish Guards would be playing, and sporting dignitaries had been invited to attend.

The teams lined up as follows:

Warrington: E. G. Fraser; B. Bevan, L. Horton, A. Naughton (capt), W. Kilbride; E. Frodsham, G. J. Helme; D. Naughton, T. McKinney, P. O'Toole, H. Bath, R. Ryan, W. McFarlane.

Leigh: J. A. Ledgard (capt); K. Holden, R. Wilson, J. Murphy, J. Gibson; A. Moore, T. O'Brien; W. Robinson, M. Dickens, S. G. Owen, P. Davies, J. Crook, J. McFarlane.

Referee: Ron Gelder (Wakefield).

Scorers:

Warrington: Tries: Bevan 2, Bath 2, McFarlane 2, Fraser, Naughton, Helme. Goals: Bath 8

Leigh: Tries. Holder, Wilson, Dickens, Goals: Ledgard 3.

The final turned out to be a very entertaining affair. Warrington's famous Australian forward, Harry Bath, turned on a masterful display both in the loose and with his goalkicking. His team proved to be too strong for the young Leigh outfit, although youth did hold out until half-time, when the score was 15-10 to Warrington.

In the second half the extra power of the Warrington side saw them run away with the match. Warrington's loose-forward Bill McFarlane, was a former Leigh player. He scored two tries in the game playing opposite his brother Joe McFarlane the Leigh loose-forward. Warrington scored nine tries, two from the great Brian Bevan and Bath also chipped in with two. Bath also slotted over eight goals as they ran out 43-15 winners.

Sadly all the records of this competition that were held by the Warrington club were destroyed in the 1980s during a fire in the Brian Bevan Stand at the old Wilderspool ground. However it is believed that the trophy presented by Associated-Rediffusion is still in existence.

As an experiment it is difficult to know if this was a success or not. The television company never repeated the exercise so from their point of view maybe it was seen as a failure. For the RFL it was just a little more exposure in the south, which was good for the game. The real winners were Warrington who retained in perpetuity the trophy they had won.

What it did do was open up a whole new issue for the RFL. Television competition had finally arrived. Both sides were looking to attract viewers and both realised the value of sport, including its ability to attract those viewers. Rugby league needed to exploit this, but not everyone in the game was agreed that it was an area into which they needed to move.

The Rugby League Television Trophy was not the first time that rugby league had been shown on television. Some four years earlier the BBC had persuaded the RFL to allow them to show a test match, against New Zealand, live on television.

The RFL had, it seems, reluctantly permitted this, so on 10 November 1951 the test was broadcast live from Station Road Swinton. A last-minute penalty saw the home side triumph 20-19 and the television moguls were hooked. A couple of months later they televised a league meeting between Wigan and Wakefield, on 12 January 1952. They then managed to negotiate the rights to show the Challenge Cup Final that year between Workington and Featherstone. Everything in the garden looked rosy, but that was not the case.

The RFL was worried about the effect that televised matches would have on attendances, not just at the televised game but also at other grounds. These worries were borne out by the attendance at Wembley for the televised Cup final. A crowd of 72,093 was more than 18,000 down on the previous season. Whether that was due to the support the two finalists had, as opposed that enjoyed by Wigan and Barrow who had contested the previous final is difficult to say, but the gate was down.

The RFL secretary, Bill Fallowfield, was firmly in the camp that said television adversely affected crowds. He managed to persuade the RFL Council not to allow the 1952-53 final to be broadcast. He was also deeply unhappy with the amount of money being offered by the BBC to cover the final and also the way the game was presented by the commentator Eddie Waring.

League championship matches were allowed to be shown but the results only added fuel to the attendance debate. Supporters were sitting at home to watch their rugby rather than going through the turnstiles. By 1953 the facts were clear to see. An international match between England and France was shown live and the total attendance at all league games that day dropped by 50 per cent.

When the 1954 World Cup Final was shown, attendances fell by more than one third. As this problem was becoming clearer, ITA burst on the scene in 1955. It was another thorn in the side for Bill Fallowfield.

The matter reached a peak in 1959, when the BBC showed the third test between Great Britain and Australia, at Central Park. The attendance of 26,089 was more than 20,000 short of the capacity for the ground and was the lowest of the test series. The first test had attracted 35,224 at Swinton and 30,029 had been at Headingley to see Great Britain win 11-10 to tie the series. The BBC paid just £1,250 for the television rights which came nowhere near covering the receipts from the missing 20,000. On the same day the Leeds, York and Bramley grounds had their lowest ever post-war attendances.

Floodlights and television seemed to go together, but the clubs were beginning to see them as an evil rather than a benefit. Television however, was here to stay and early in 1965 the RFL decided to emulate the experiment carried out by Associated Rediffusion some 10 years earlier.

In May 1965, the RFL Council, which by now had a Television Sub-Committee, discussed television rights. Widnes's Mr Davies said that his club felt that contracts for televising games should be negotiated by the clubs rather than the RFL. However, this idea was rejected. It was agreed that county cup games could be televised.

Of more significance, it was reported to the Council that the BBC had asked the RFL to organise a midweek floodlit competition to start in October 1965. They offered £9,000 for 12 midweek games to be shown on BBC2, which was starting to broadcast in the north at that time. The idea was accepted. At the June Council meeting, it was agreed that 11 matches would be played for the £9,000.

Attitudes were changing at both the clubs and the RFL and also in broadcasting. Michael Peacock was replaced as controller of BBC2, by the then David Attenborough, now Sir David. BBC2 had been launched in April 1964, but Attenborough brought a more innovative outlook to the new channel. When approached by executives about the prospect of showing rugby league under floodlights in the middle of the week he responded enthusiastically. Hence was born the BBC2 Floodlit Trophy.

The new competition along with the prize money on offer stimulated the clubs into action and caused them to approach the RFL with a view to the governing body funding, or part funding, those clubs who installed lighting. The floodlighting era blossomed from one club in 1964, to 22 clubs by 1974 who had installed floodlights at their grounds. Ironically one of the clubs now without lighting was the club who had begun the whole affair, Bradford Northern.

Bradford Northern's lights had been damaged by a storm in 1960. The club was in desperate straits and could not afford to repair them. Floodlit rugby league was not restored to Odsal until 1978, after a fundraising campaign by the supporters to pay for the new lights.

The stage was set for a revolution in floodlit rugby league. It was once again a fledgling organisation, BBC2, that set about bolstering its standing by linking up with sport. It was a relationship which was to last longer than the relationship with the electricity companies back in 1878. The BBC2 Floodlit Trophy ran for 15 years, from 1965 through to 1980.

The effect it had on club decisions to install floodlighting at their grounds is seen from the table below, which shows the season during which each listed club introduced lights:

1964-65: Swinton, St Helens.
1965-66: Castleford, Oldham, Warrington, Widnes, Salford.
1966-67: Rochdale Hornets, Leeds, Barrow.
1967-68: Halifax, Hull, Wigan, Hull KR, Wakefield Trinity, Keighley, Huddersfield.
1973-74: Bramley, Dewsbury, Whitehaven.
1974-75: New Hunslet

Even then, some long-established clubs, such as Batley, York, Workington Town and Featherstone Rovers did not have floodlights.

In June 1965, the RFL Council had considered applications for loans to clubs to enable them to install floodlights. It was agreed that 75 per cent of the cost per club could be met, up to £8,000. Castleford, Widnes, Wigan, Oldham, Warrington and Leeds had all applied for loans, and Castleford's, at £6,000, had already been agreed.

Another spin-off from the growth of floodlighting in the game was playing matches on Friday nights. Salford was one of the first clubs to take this initiative, and some others followed.

The BBC2 Floodlit Trophy

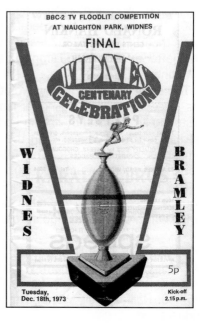

Programmes from three Finals: St Helens's second win in 1975; Bramley's famous victory in the afternoon in 1973 and the last Final: A sell-out Hull derby match.

(Courtesy St Helens RLFC & Alex Service, Widnes Vikings RLFC and Hull FC respectively)

17. The BBC2 Floodlit Trophy

As with many innovations in rugby league, the BBC2 Floodlit Trophy came in with a whisper rather than tumultuous acclaim. The competition was launched in 1965 when just eight clubs entered. In fact only seven clubs entered but the authorities persuaded Leeds to make the number up to eight. *The Rugby Leaguer* on 27 August 1965 did not see the announcement of the new competition as being something special. In a round up of close-season happenings it wrote about the BBC2 initiative: "Announced that £9,000 was to be paid by the BBC for the televising of 11 matches in the inaugural RL Floodlit Competition due to start early in October. Five Lancashire and one Yorkshire club (Castleford) are to be involved."

That was all that was written about it in the sport's newspaper. From then to the competition starting the number of clubs went from six to eight. Those taking part were: Castleford, Leeds, Leigh, Oldham, St. Helens, Swinton, Warrington and Widnes. Because Leeds did not install their floodlights until September 1966, they had to play their matches away from home.

The tournament followed a similar format to the 1955 one run by Associated-Rediffusion. From the preliminary play-off matches the four teams with the best match points and points for-and-against difference would progress through to a semi-final draw. The full results of matches played in this first competition were:

Castleford 7 Leeds 7   St Helens 21 Leeds 9
Leigh 13 Warrington 9   Swinton 21 Oldham 5
Oldham 4 Castleford 6   Warrington 10 Widnes 20
St Helens 25 Leigh 19   Widnes 19 Swinton 8

The four qualifiers for the semi-finals were:
Widnes (+21)
St Helens (+18)
Swinton (+5)
Castleford (+2).

Semi finals
St Helens 9 Swinton 5   Widnes 9 Castleford 12

Final
St Helens 0 Castleford 4

The first game of the competition was played at Knowsley Road on Tuesday 5 October 1965. The programme notes give some insight as to the clubs' thinking towards the competition and the effects of television: "Tonight we [St Helens] play our first game in the BBC2

Television Contest. It is appropriate that we have Leigh here for our first game, for our visitors were the first rugby league club to take a step in the direction of evening rugby. Like so many people of vision they were years in advance of their time.

On all sides they will be receiving belated recognition of their foresight. Those of us who follow years after were compelled by the pressure of falling gates to try to meet the competition of Television on Saturday afternoons. We are finding that Friday nights and Monday nights are providing the gates we used to get ten years ago..."

The BBC *Grandstand* programme on Saturday afternoons was proving to be so popular that the clubs and the authorities felt it was affecting their gates. Their answer was to switch to night matches to combat the effects. Ironically it was television that was helping them towards that goal.

The clubs were desperately trying to battle against the social changes that took place in the 1960s. Gates were falling from the post-war highs, revenue was consequently down as well, so something had to be done. Whether the BBC realised this or not is unknown, but they took advantage of the situation in the game to start their competition which ran for 15 years.

The rest of the media was not over-impressed with the first competition, feeling that it was not really a competitive contest, not like the League or the established Lancashire and Yorkshire Cups and the Challenge Cup.

The final between St Helens and Castleford played at Knowsley Road on Tuesday 14 December 1965 attracted little coverage. Even *The Rugby Leaguer* in its issue the following Friday deemed it worthy of only five paragraphs:

"Against all the odds, but deservedly if only for their superior handling in heavy conditions Castleford brought off a great victory at St Helens on Tuesday in the final of the BBC Floodlit competition.

The match was decided by penalty goals. Ron Willett Castleford's marksman who was completely out of touch in the previous match, a home defeat by Halifax, this time was on the mark with his first shot and got another fine goal in the second half.

Len Killeen, hero of so many St Helens successes this season gave a nightmare display of kicking and failed with six chances.

The league leaders played in a cramped style. If either of their wingmen got the ball it was by accident and this was despite Dagnall's success in the scrums and Prosser's quick service. Murphy gave a useful and controlled display for Saints who were let down by a general habit among the forwards of trying to get through alone. Edwards, a fine runner of the ball, was one of Castleford's big successes at full back.

Hardisty was a tower of strength in the second half. Small did well at loose forward and Ab Terry whose career began at St Helens many seasons ago was another useful performer."

Castleford: D. Edwards; C. Battye, M. Battye, R. Willett, T. Briggs; A. Hardisty, R. Millward; A. E. Terry, J. Ward, C. Dickinson, W. Bryant, P. Small, J. Taylor.

St Helens: F. Barrow; K. T. van Vollenhoven, D. Wood, W. Benyon, L. M. A. Killen; A. J. Murphy, R. Prosser; R. French, R. Dagnall, C. H. Watson, M. J. Hicks, J. Mantle, C. D. Laughton.

Referee: L. Gant (Wrenthorpe)

Scorer:

Castleford: Goals: R. Willett (2).

That was their entire write up of the final. It is amazing just how this competition grew from such small beginnings and helped set the pattern for the future of the game.

The Rugby Leaguer was less than convinced about televising rugby league, On 19 November 1965 it said: "What is the real future of floodlit football in the rugby league game? That may be a question no one can answer but it need not prevent our asking it, with the aim of getting our clubs and their controllers to look just a little further than even next season or the one that follows that."

The article went on to cover various issues, such as society's changing social structure, and whether supporters would come out on a cold night to watch rugby. If floodlighting was doing nothing else, it was getting all concerned in the game to think about the future. More importantly it seemed to be attracting both supporters to the grounds and viewers to switch to the new programme.

During the competition's first year the 11 matches that were played attracted 74,149 spectators, giving an average attendance of 6,741. This pleased the RFL, and the average would have been much better had not an Oldham game been played on the foulest of nights attracting a crowd of fewer than 1,000. The two best attended matches were the first and the last, both involving St Helens. Their game against Leigh attracted 12,592 while the final against Castleford attracted 11,510.

It would seem everyone concerned with the new competition was happy with the results and more clubs wanted to join the competition. However, televised coverage did cause problems for some players. League legend Roger Millward recalled in his autobiography:

"I can remember playing Widnes in the floodlit cup, a competition that was played on a Tuesday night. I was on nights, my shift started at 10pm and finished at 5.15am the next day. Hull was a good 55 miles from Castleford... It was a good game and we beat Widnes, a good result for us... I left Hull immediately after changing. The next morning the 'electrical boss' was at work at 5.15 a.m. which I thought was a little unusual...

'You did well last night Roger', he said. Which I thought was a bit funny, as he was not a rugby fan. 'Yes, we played well and everything seemed to go for us', I replied.

'No Roger, not the result of the game, I watched you on television at 9pm and you had clocked on for 10pm' he exclaimed. Deathly silence followed. My friend Allen Williams and I had been rumbled. 'Just be careful he said.' "

One of his mates, it seems, clocked on for him while he was away playing. Unfortunately his boss was watching the match on his television and wondered just how Roger the Dodger could possibly be in two places at the same time.

In the trophy's second season, three new clubs entered: Barrow, Rochdale Hornets and Salford. As a consequence of this the rugby authorities instigated a preliminary round over two legs to eliminate three clubs. The three unlucky losers were Leigh, Rochdale and Salford.

The rules for qualifying for the semi-finals remained the same, albeit a somewhat tortuous system. Teams winning all their matches qualified automatically, otherwise it was the best for-and-against points record. Should five teams win all their matches then the four with the best scoring record away from home would qualify.

The competition was used by the RFL to try out new rules without encroaching on the league fixtures. They tested a system put forward by New Zealand that each team should have four tackles before having a scrum. It was explained thus by the RFL: "To allow one team three play-the-balls after which if the ball has not been 'played' by the opposition a scrum is formed. The term 'played' in this context means 'intentionally handled or kicked' rebounds or ricochet of the ball from an opponent does not count as being 'played'. When a scrum is formed after three play-the-balls the side which was not in possession of the ball shall put the ball in and have the loose head."

Oldham versus Barrow was the first match under the new system. There were 44 scrums, 15 from the new rule, and others because players kicked for touch after two tackles.

It was also decided that the defence would retire five yards back from the play-the-ball rather than the three then in use. Finally the BBC introduced a man-of-the-match award with a cash prize. The

Left: Roger Millward – one of the players who became nationally known through his appearances on BBC2 – even if it did cause him problems clocking on for the night shift occasionally.
(Photo: Courtesy Robert Gate)

Right: The BBC2 Floodlit Trophy
(Photo: Courtesy John Riding)

winner was selected by the viewers via the *Radio Times*. Viewers filled in a coupon in the *Radio Times* which they posted, and the next week the player voted man-of-the-match was invited to the televised game and presented with a cheque on air at half-time.

One game in particular that season that convinced everyone involved in the game that the four tackle rule was a success. It was in the first round proper of the competition and involved local rivals Castleford and Leeds. They fought out an 11-11 draw, the second time in the competition they had played out a draw. It was the then seemingly breathtaking pace at which the match was played that amazed everyone.

Not everyone was in favour however; a number of players were canvassed after playing under the new rules. The views of six club captains were:

Peter Smethurst (Oldham): "I'll finish if the rule comes in."

Ray French (St. Helens): "I don't like it at all and the feeling is general among Saints players. It's like touch rugby and the real essence goes out of the game."

Ken Gower (Swinton): "I thought the rule was terrible. There isn't sufficient time to settle down with the ball and do something constructive."

Johnny Noon (Rochdale Hornets): "You don't know whether you are coming or going. There is a lot of end-to-end stuff but most of it is aimless. It brings a game very much like tig and pass."

Arthur Hughes (Salford): "Neither impressed nor disillusioned."

Jim Challinor (Barrow): "I was against it immediately after Tuesday's game but I would not like to reach a conclusive verdict quickly."

The supporters, however, were greatly in favour of the new rules and it was this which led the RFL to decide on 26 October to introduce the four-tackle rule for all matches with immediate effect if both clubs agreed. Floodlit rugby certainly had arrived as a result of this decision. In December the clubs unanimously agreed to adopt the rule for all matches. The same meeting agreed another momentous change: matches could be played on Sundays if both teams agreed.

While the majority of people connected to the game were greatly in favour of the introduction of the four tackle rule, the most important people, the players, were not. Many still favoured the unlimited tackles that allowed a team to build pressure in order to score tries. However, it was slow and outmoded and supporters wanted to see a faster sport, the four-tackle rule gave them that.

Ray French, ironically today the BBC television rugby league commentator, was scathing of the experiment 40 years later: "The whole experiment was basically the brainchild of the then secretary of the rugby league, Bill Fallowfield. He was always going on about the predictability of the play-the-ball. In fact in 1961 he organised a game between a British XIII and a French XIII. The British team, with the exception of the hooker Bill Sayer, was made up of players who had been signed from rugby union. I played and we had the likes of van Vollenhoven, Allan Skeen, Renilson and Bev Risman.

The rules for the game said we had to release the ball every tackle. The result was a shambles, players simply could not keep up with the pace of the game. The idea turned out to be a failure and was scrapped.

However, when the idea for four tackles came up in 1966 Fallowfield was all in favour of it, the players certainly were not. It was all too frantic and frenetic with no structure. You could not exert any real pressure on the opposition and it all seemed pointless. After two tackles you were thinking, 'what do we do now?'

It actually ended the careers of a lot of player and not just those who were getting on in years. There was no room for the ball-playing front row forward or a loose-forward. You could not really afford to take a tackle on your own line, in an attempt to clear the danger. The game became all about field position rather than developing pressure and letting the backs score the tries. For me the whole game became a mish-mash sort of affair."

Another player caught up in this experiment was Wakefield Trinity's Neil Fox, one of the game's legends. He was not really a fan of the change either: "When they brought in the four tackle rule all of the players really had to learn how to play a different game. You could not go onto the field with a game plan as such. You had no time to work out moves, it was ridiculous really. The six tackles we have now is not ideal, but it is better than the four tackle rule.

We went from a game where the forwards would make the hard yards from their own try line up to the 25-yard line, then the backs would get the ball and they would put a move on. Now we had a scrum and the scrum half may get tackled and you had three tackles to try to work something. If you look at the six tackle rule today it makes all teams play the same way. They have five drives and then it is either a grubber over the line, or a high kick to the wingman.

Players were running around like headless chickens when the new rule came in, they did not know what to do. I saw much less of the ball once we switched to four tackles than when it was unlimited tackles. Certainly my team, Trinity, had less success under the new rules. Castleford on the other hand loved it, they became the 'classy Cas' that we know today as a result of the change.

The RFL often changed things half-way through a season. It was the same with this rule, we started the season with unlimited tackles and switched to four tackles half-way through. I am not all that sure that the fans loved the changes, I know I didn't."

By the second season, the number of matches involved in the competition increased from 11 to 17, with 11 teams taking part, but the BBC prize money of £9,000 for the clubs did not grow. The television viewing figures in the second year of the competition also showed that viewing numbers were up.

In the Floodlit Trophy it did not matter to Castleford whether they were playing under the unlimited tackle rule or the four tackle rule, they just kept winning. They retained the trophy at the end of the year, beating Swinton 7-2 in another low-scoring final.

As the competition's third year began, 17 clubs participated. Halifax, Huddersfield, Hull, Hull KR, Keighley, Wakefield and Wigan entered the fray. Also the rules were to change once again. It was decided that the competition would be run on the same lines as the Challenge Cup. It would be a straight knock out, with clubs being drawn out of the hat, with the semi-finals and final played on a neutral ground.

The BBC also introduced a new innovation: colour television and they wanted to broadcast some rugby league in the new format. This meant that clubs had to upgrade their lighting system to cope with the higher demands of colour television. What it meant was that rugby league clubs, had in some cases, floodlighting which was better than that of neighbouring association football clubs.

Once again it made little difference to Castleford who won the competition again. They met Leigh in the final and true to form came away with a narrow 8-5 victory. The floodlit competition led to Castleford becoming the 'Classy Cas' of the 1970s and 1980s. They got a taste winning finals, going on to victory in the Yorkshire Cup and the Challenge Cup in later years.

The competition continued to go from strength to strength. What was pleasing to both the BBC and the RFL was the success of some of the smaller clubs in the league. Rochdale Hornets reached the final, narrowly losing out 8-2 to St Helens in 1971. Bramley, sadly no longer in the game's professional ranks, won the trophy beating Widnes 15-7 in a shock 1973-74 final. It was the year of the Israeli Yom Kippur War and the oil-producing nations in the middle east introduced an oil embargo on the west in retaliation for western support of Israel. There was a 50 mph speed restriction introduced in this country in an attempt to save fuel. There was also a shortage of coal and power-station output was reduced, partly due to industrial action by the miners. Consequently the government placed an embargo on floodlit sport. As a result the final and a number of other matches were played in the afternoon, not under floodlights.

It was Bramley's first final in their history and on the way there they accounted for the mighty St Helens. The government's floodlighting embargo seemed to have helped rather than hindered the club and it was their finest hour when they travelled home with the trophy.

The Bramley coach Arthur Keegan had a simple game plan for the final, which had worked well all season, so he had no need to change it. The plan was to capitalise on every mistake that Widnes made. By all accounts Widnes made plenty during the game and Bramley took full advantage. Bramley did so without much possession either. It was only in the eighth minute of the second half that their hooker, Firth, managed to win his first heel in the scrum. In those days the scrum-half had to put the ball in the middle of the tunnel and scrums were contested, unlike today.

Widnes's woes began as early as the third minute when Blackwood dropped the ball behind his 25-yard line. Bramley pounced and wingman Austin crossed in the corner. He then coolly slotted over the conversion from the touchline. All Widnes could muster for all their efforts was two penalty goals.

In the second half when Bramley brought on Sampson they began to enjoy more possession, and they used it well. Sampson went over for a try and John Wolford added a drop-goal later to take the visitors clear. For Widnes, Macko pulled a try back but it was too little too late. When Goodchild was controversially awarded a penalty try the trophy was on its way to McLaren Field much to the surprise of the rest of the rugby league world.

As the tournament progressed, sadly its fortunes began to wane. The introduction of the Players No.6 Trophy in 1976, played at weekends, and featured on television, in its own way sounded the death knell for the floodlit tournament. It continued to be played but to ever decreasing audiences. Perhaps the novelty of going to watch rugby league in the evening was wearing off?

The final season of the competition, 1979-80, brought together fierce local rivals Hull and Hull KR in a final watched by 18,500 at The Boulevard and millions on television. The black and whites ran out winners 13-3 in a pulsating match. Afterwards, the match, the BBC, in conjunction with the RFL, decided to drop the competition and a floodlit outlet for sport was closed off.

It seems that the new controller of BBC2, Brian Wenham, was more interested in the arts and big-budget sport than the perceived narrow and parochial game of rugby league. Wenham felt that rugby league did not fit into his view of what BBC2 programmes should be presenting and the type of viewer he wanted to attract. Also the BBC pointed out that they were having to provide extra lighting at the floodlit games because the existing lights at the grounds were not good enough to allow broadcasts to go ahead in colour. This was becoming more and more costly for the television company.

The RFL on their part was happy to go along with this view. The feeling was that television affected gates at other matches. The sports programme *Grandstand* was asked to stop advertising in advance which match would be televised and television viewers were only able to watch the match after 20 minutes of the first half had been played.

The authorities came to the conclusion that there were too many games and it was becoming impossible to squeeze them into a single season. The obvious games to cut were the county cups and the BBC2 trophy. The feeling was the competition had run its course, attendances were falling and it was a competition which was no longer the money spinner it had once been.

The John Player Trophy was attracting fans whereas the floodlit competition was losing fans. When the BBC hinted that the cost of staging such matches was becoming prohibitive it gave the RFL an avenue of escape and they decided to pull the plug on the Floodlit Trophy. There was also another reason for dispersing with the competition: the BBC would not allow any form of sponsorship for the tournament so clubs could not augment lost revenue from the gates.

Ironically they did so after what turned out the biggest money spinning match in its history, the Hull verses Hull KR final. But gates prior to that had all been down on previous years. A number of seemingly small issues came together at one time and meant the demise of the Floodlit Trophy. A few years later there was a hue and cry when the authorities ditched the Lancashire and Yorkshire County Cups for similar reasons.

The Floodlit Trophy had produced new stars. Players such as Roger Millward and others found their first success on a national stage in this competition. Clubs, particularly the smaller ones, also found success in the new competition.

It is true that there is nothing new in sport and nowhere is this more so than in floodlit rugby league. Today the fans take for granted that both rugby and association football will be on their television screens on any evening. It is hard to see in the future the inception of another floodlit competition in the style of either the ITA or BBC2 concepts because floodlit matches are now a normal part of any club's fixtures.

Some clubs did not install lights in time to take part in the floodlit competition, but did so later. The list below shows the season that other clubs installed lights:

1983-84: Featherstone Rovers
1989-90: Doncaster, York
1990-91: Workington Town
1991-92: Batley

Some clubs played on grounds which already had lights, such as Cardiff City, Carlisle (at Brunton Park), Chorley, Fulham (at Craven Cottage and Crystal Palace), Kent Invicta, Sheffield Eagles and Trafford Borough. Others who moved grounds, such as Highfield and Nottingham City had lights at some grounds but not others. But small clubs could survive without lights – Fulham played at The Polytechnic Stadium in Chiswick from 1985 to 1990 without floodlights.

Even grounds with floodlights could have problems. In 1999 the London Broncos were playing at Harlequins RFC's The Stoop. Planning permission problems, since resolved, meant that the ground's floodlights could not be used on a Saturday night, when Sky televised a match in April. Inadequate temporary floodlights were used, with older fans recalling the early days of floodlighting at non-league football grounds with light and dark areas of the pitch. A miserable evening with continual rain did not help their enjoyment of the game.

Now with Sky and terrestrial television promoting British rugby league to even greater heights, it is easy to forget the very humble beginnings of floodlit sport some 129 years ago. Those pioneers of both science and sport were in part responsible for the way sport is watched and played today, and gave us something that is taken for granted. They really did manage to 'snuff out the Moon'.

There is, however, yet another little black cloud on the horizon, for the game, and sport; high-definition television. This, if it takes off as the terrestrial and satellite broadcasters would wish, would leave many rugby league clubs potentially facing the prospect of having to improve dramatically the quality of the floodlighting they currently have, as in the 1970s, when the introduction of colour television caused clubs to do the same. Then the BBC paid out to improve the quality of light produced by the existing floodlights at grounds. High-definition television may well cause similar upgrades to be necessary at sports grounds, but at what cost, and to whom? Only time will resolve that particular dilemma.

The aim of this book has been to help set the record straight on misconceptions about floodlit association football and rugby. Perhaps those watching floodlit sport should give a little thanks to all those who helped to dig the well over the last century and more.

Appendix: The BBC2 Floodlit Trophy Final results

14 Dec 1965	Castleford 4 St Helens 0	at Knowsley Rd	11,510
20 Dec 1966	Castleford 7 Swinton 2	at Wheldon Rd	8,986
16 Jan 1968	Castleford 8 Leigh 5	at Headingley	9,525
17 Dec 1968	Wigan 7 St Helens 4	at Central Park	13,479
16 Dec 1969	Leigh 11 Wigan 6	at Central Park	12,234
15 Dec 1970	Leeds 9 St Helens 5	at Headingley	7,612
14 Dec 1971	St Helens 8 Rochdale H 2	at Knowsley Rd	9,300
19 Dec 1972	Leigh 5 Widnes 0	at Central Park	4,872
18 Dec 1973	Bramley 15 Widnes 7	at Naughton Park	4,000
17 Dec 1974	Salford 0 Warrington 0	at The Willows	4,473
28 Jan 1975 (Rep)	Salford 10 Warrington 5	at Wilderspool	5,778
16 Dec 1975	St Helens 22 Dewsbury 2	at Knowsley Rd	4,000
14 Dec 1976	Castleford 12 Leigh 4	at Hilton Park	5,417
13 Dec 1977	Hull KR 26 St Helens 11	at Craven Park	10,099
12 Dec 1978	Widnes 13 St Helens 7	at Knowsley Rd	10,250
18 Dec 1979	Hull 13 Hull K.R. 3	at The Boulevard	18,500

NB The 1973 match was not played under floodlights due to the restrictions on floodlit matches at this time.

This is a book about ordinary people going about their business in an ordinary manner, in extraordinary times. What makes them special, if in fact they are special, is simply that they were sportsmen. Each of the 13 written about in this book was a rugby player. Some were internationals in one or other code, League or Union. They all had one thing in common, they were to lose their lives fighting for King and country.

Since its publication it has been instrumental in uncovering evidence of two other professional rugby league players who won the VC in World War One: Thomas Steele (Broughton Rangers) and Thomas Bryan (Castleford.)

It is available from
Tom Mather
20 Chandler's Rest
Lytham
Lytham St Anne's
FY8 5AL
Price £8.95 (Inc. postage)
Cheques payable to Tom Mather

Rugby league books from
London League Publications Ltd

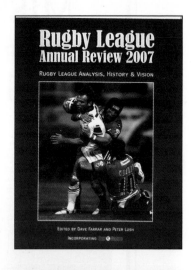

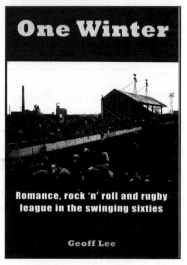